Men and Women Are from Eden

A Study Guide to John Paul II's Theology of the Body

Mary Healy

PUBLISHED BY ST. ANTHONY MESSENGER PRESS
CINCINNATI, OHIO

Nihil Obstat:
Rev. Isidore Dixon
Censor Deputatus

Imprimatur:
Reverend Msgr. Godfrey Mosley
Vicar General for the Archdiocese of Washington
March 9, 2005

The nihil obstat and imprimatur are official declarations that a book or pamphlet is free of doctrinal or moral error. No implication is contained therein that those who have granted the nihil obstat and the imprimatur agree with the content, opinions or statements expressed.

Cover design by Mark Sullivan
Book design by Phillips Robinette, O.F.M.

LIBRARY OF CONGRESS CATALOGING-IN-PUBLICATION DATA

Healy, Mary, 1964-
    Men and women are from Eden : a study guide to John Paul II's Theology of the body / Mary Healy.
        p. cm.
    Includes index.
    ISBN 0-86716-700-9 (pbk. : alk. paper)
    1. John Paul II, Pope, 1920- Theology of the body. 2. Body, Human—Religious aspects—Catholic Church. 3. Catholic Church—Doctrines. I. Title.
    BX1795.B63J6434 2005
    233'.5—dc22

                              2005006027

ISBN-13: 978-0-87616-700-9
ISBN-10: 0-86716-700-9

Published by Servant Books, an imprint of St. Anthony Messenger Press.
28 W. Liberty St.
Cincinnati, OH 45202
www.ServantBooks.org

Printed in the United States of America

Printed on acid-free paper

        09 10 11 12 7 6 5 4

To John Paul II the Great
1920–2005
Faithful servant of Christ,
defender of human life,
papa to the whole world.

ACKNOWLEDGMENTS

This book began as a series of talks on the theology of the body given at Mother of God Community in Gaithersburg, Maryland. I am very grateful to the other two speakers, Fr. Francis Martin and Dr. John Grabowski, for sharing their insights on the pope's teaching and allowing me to incorporate material from their talks in this study guide.

The inspiration for this book is in large part the fruit of the beautiful example of Christian marriage provided by the members of Mother of God Community and by my parents, family and neighbors in Munsonville, New Hampshire. I thank them for their witness to the power of Christ's grace.

I would also like to thank Lynn Cothern, Tony Bosnick and my editor, Cindy Cavnar, for their encouragement and their suggestions, which greatly improved the manuscript.

Contents

INTRODUCTION

Popular wisdom tells us that "Men are from Mars, women are from Venus."[1] This humorous maxim does seem to be borne out by experience. Deep in every human heart is inscribed the desire to love and be loved in an intimate, lasting relationship. How many people spend their lives pursuing this desire! Yet many find it elusive, struggling with romantic relationships only to end up in disillusionment, conflict or emotional distance.

The desire for love touches on the very core of our identity as human beings. As Pope John Paul II once said,

> Man cannot live without love. He remains a being that is incomprehensible for himself, his life is senseless, if love is not revealed to him, if he does not encounter love, if he does not experience it and make it his own, if he does not participate intimately in it.[2]

Bookshelves are full of self-help manuals offering answers to our longings for love and our challenges in relating to others, especially those of the opposite sex. Many of these books provide valuable advice. But John Paul II invites us to something more foundational. If we want to discover the real meaning of man and woman, and the reasons why we relate to one another as we do, we must probe not only our psychological makeup or our typical behaviors but, more importantly, what God has revealed about our ultimate origins.

God continually calls us to go "back to the beginning"— to rediscover *his* wonderful plan for humanity. Only by understanding and living according to that original plan can we find the answer to our searching and have a restored hope for relationships of deep, authentic love. The secret of man and woman is found not on different planets but in the biblical account of the first couple, created by God and placed in the garden of Paradise at the dawn of human history. Men and women are from Eden!

A NEW VISION

In our time God has provided a marvelous vehicle for this rediscovery of his original plan: the writings of John Paul II known as "the theology of the body." These writings are a fresh and profoundly original approach to the church's teaching on love, sex and marriage. They give us a whole new vision for understanding who we are as men and women and how we can experience the happiness for which God destined us.

The pope's message is truly a countercultural one. If we look at the world around us, the state of affairs with respect to men, women, sex and marriage could be described as anything but Paradise. The prevailing philosophy, "I can do what I want with my body," has led to a cultural landscape littered with broken families, lost human dignity, lonely individuals and deep moral confusion. We face the specter of even greater disasters: human beings created in the lab specifically for the purpose of exploitation and destruction, a massive international sex tourism network, a multibillion-dollar porn industry, an escalating attack on God's plan for the family.

It is no exaggeration to say that sex and marriage are in a meltdown—a crisis perhaps greater than at any other time in history. And in the midst of it all, Pope John Paul II had the boldness to say that the answer is found in Eden—that the joy of lasting, true love experienced in the first marriage before the Fall is possible here and now.

Is this pure idealism on the part of an elderly celibate male? His critics say it is. But those who have studied and put into practice the theology of the body say this teaching is realistic, it is empowering, and it gives them a whole new vision for their lives—whether they are young singles, older couples, families struggling to raise their kids or those suffering the pain of divorce or widowhood.

Long before he was pope, Karol Wojtyla was friends with and counseled hundreds of married couples. He dealt with virtually every human struggle in the confessional. He was thinking, writing and reflecting philosophically on the meaning of the human person, the body, love and sexuality at a time when it was very unusual for a prelate to do so. As a young priest and bishop his views were considered avant-garde and daring.

No pope ever wrote as deeply, or as much, on human love as has John Paul II. The outcome of his reflections, the theology of the body, is God's wonderful providence for our time. This is in part because the old arguments for the church's moral teaching simply were not adequate to meet the challenges of the third millennium. It is not that they were false; they simply were not convincing enough for people living in a dramatically changed social context. New problems needed a new vision, a new framework and a new vocabulary to make the church's teaching compelling and attractive, to unveil the radiance of truth.

John Paul II presents us with this new vision—which, insofar as it is an unfolding of biblical truths, is not really new. The pope says, in effect, that there is something glorious in God's plan for human love and sexuality, though not in the way the world understands it. And the all-important but often undervalued key to unlocking this plan is the human *body*.

THE TIME BOMB

The pope first presented the theology of the body as a series in his weekly addresses (general audiences) between 1979 and 1984, the first five years of his pontificate. These addresses have been collected and published as *The Theology of the Body: Human Love in the Divine Plan* (Pauline Books and Media, 1997). One might reasonably wonder why, after more than two decades, this timely and desperately needed teaching is still virtually unknown to most Catholics. There are at least two major reasons.

First, the John Paul's addresses are not what one would call light reading. They can tend to be somewhat abstract. Moreover, most of us are used to Western or classical Greek reasoning, which could be described as linear: Point A leads to point B, which leads to point C and so on. The pope's reasoning, on the other hand, is Slavic. It could be described as spiral and is actually much closer to biblical thought. He comes back to the same topic again and again, but always on a different level, going deeper. It takes time to become accustomed to this way of proceeding.

Second, for the last generation there has been an atmosphere of dissent in many Catholic institutions. Many universities, diocesan and parish religious education offices, and schools have been less than enthusiastic about the church's authentic moral teaching, especially in the area of sexuality.

This situation has improved considerably in recent years, in part because of the John Paul II Institutes now set up around the world, where the theology of the body is studied in depth and applied to contemporary moral issues.[3]

The purpose of this study guide is to contribute to the spread of the John Paul's teaching in a form that laypeople can readily understand and appropriate. It does so especially from a biblical perspective because, as we will see, the pope's teaching is profoundly biblical.

This guide also has an evangelistic purpose, since the theology of the body is intrinsically evangelistic. A healing of minds in regard to the body and sexuality can be a powerful instrument in leading people to Christ. In fact, it is hardly possible to understand and accept the theology of the body without gaining a deeper reverence for God and his magnificent plan. Nor is it possible to live this teaching without turning to a deeper reliance on the power of Christ's cross and the Holy Spirit. The theology of the body is good news!

Karol Wojtyla recognized long ago that in the war between good and evil in our day, it is these matters relating to the body, sex, marriage and the family that are *the* battleground. We who are followers of Christ have an immense obligation to engage in this battle. This study guide will give you the tools to begin to apply the theology of the body to your life and to share it with others so that they, too, can experience the beauty of God's plan. Papal biographer George Weigel has predicted that the theology of the body is a "kind of theological time bomb destined to go off, with dramatic consequences, sometime in the Third Millennium of the Church."[4] We all have a share in setting off that explosion!

PREPARE FOR ADVENTURE!

This guide is designed for use in parishes, communities, small groups and similar settings, as well as for individual study. Apart from this booklet itself, all that is needed is a Bible and a journal or notebook to write in. Those who desire more in-depth study can also refer to the *Catechism of the Catholic Church (CCC)* and to the text of *The Theology of the Body*.[5]

Each chapter in this guide presents a part of John Paul II's teaching in a form that can be readily understood and applied to real life. At the end of each chapter is a "Study Tools" section, which provides references to Scripture and church teaching, the corresponding general audiences, a glossary of key concepts, questions for personal prayer and small group discussion, an idea for practical application, and a Bible verse to commit to memory. The terms defined in the glossary are highlighted in bold when they first occur in the text. Thoughtfully working through the questions and, ideally, discussing your answers with others are keys to a deeply personal and life-changing assimilation of the theology of the body.

When using this guide in a small group setting, it is helpful (though not essential) to have a facilitator who has some experience in leading discussions. The facilitator plays the important role of creating a warm and relaxed atmosphere, and of guiding the conversation so that everyone has time to share and feels that their answers are genuinely appreciated. At the same time, the conversation needs to stay on track and focus not only on people's subjective responses but on learning the objective truths of the theology of the body. An attitude of genuine enthusiasm and love for God's Word and for the teachings of the church will set a positive tone for the whole group.

The questions provided at the end of each chapter range from the informational and interpretive to the personal. All participants should be encouraged to engage at a level where they feel comfortable, and no one should feel pressured to share on any given question.

A suggested format for small group meetings is to begin with some informal conversation to allow people to get to know one another. Then pray for a few minutes in a form suited to the group, asking the Lord for his presence and wisdom to help you understand and apply what you are learning. Then spend a short time summarizing the material in the chapter, section by section. Finally, discuss the questions provided at the end of the chapter.

The discussion will be most fruitful if participants have read the chapter during the previous week and written down their answers to the questions. Some groups may want to break into smaller groups or pairs for the more personal questions. If the group meets regularly to work through this study guide, relationships of trust will develop, and people will feel free to share on a more personal level. Close the meeting with another prayer, asking God for the grace to bring what you have learned into the week.

Those who are interested in learning more are encouraged to supplement their use of this guide with the resources for further study provided in the back. If a question regarding church teaching or the meaning of a passage arises that the group cannot answer, simply put it on hold until there is an opportunity to research the issue through outside reading or by speaking to someone knowledgeable about it.

Delving into the theology of the body is an adventure! You will find that these teachings stretch your mind, deepen your understanding of God's Word, challenge some of your assumed ways of thinking and inspire you to love more generously. The most important equipment to bring to the study of the theology of the body is simply an attitude of prayer and a heart open to the truth, which God alone can bring to life within us.

Chapter One

BACK TO THE BEGINNING

John Paul II begins his teaching on the **theology of the body** in a surprising way. Rather than the lofty opening passage we might expect, the pope takes as his starting point an episode from the Gospel of Matthew about divorce. His focus, however, is not divorce itself but rather an inconspicuous phrase to which he returns again and again during his next several addresses. The phrase is "from the beginning."

> And Pharisees came up to him and tested him by asking, "Is it lawful to divorce one's wife for any cause?" He answered, "Have you not read that he who made them *from the beginning* made them male and female, and said, 'For this reason a man shall leave his father and mother and be joined to his wife, and the two shall become one flesh'? So they are no longer two but one. What therefore God has joined together, let no man put asunder." They said to him, "Why then did Moses command one to give a certificate of divorce, and to put her away?" He said to them, "For your hardness of heart Moses allowed you to divorce your wives, but *from the beginning* it was not so. And I say to you: whoever divorces his wife, except for unchastity, and marries another, commits adultery."
>
> —MATTHEW 19:3–9, emphasis added

In this scene the Pharisees seek to trap Jesus by asking him a question about the legal grounds for divorce. If he says, "Yes, it is lawful," they can accuse him of moral laxity. If he says no, they can accuse him of being a harsh rigorist.

But Jesus refuses to reply on their level. Instead he points them back to Genesis, to God's original intention for humanity. Only by discovering that original plan, he indicates, can we understand our own situation and find the answers to our questions about sex and marriage. To understand who we are now, we must first go back to Eden.

But Jesus also indicates that something has changed. Now that he has come, the situation that prevailed under the law of Moses no longer applies. Hardness of heart and the resulting family breakdown are no longer the inevitable consequences of sin! There is a new phase, a new reality in place, with a new power enabling us to experience what God intended. Otherwise, there would be no point in going back to "the beginning," except to mourn what we had lost forever. Because Christ has come, the innocence and beauty of God's original plan can be restored and, in fact, something even greater gained.

Later in his teachings the pope looks closely at another passage in Matthew (22:23–33), which serves as a second reference point for the theology of the body. This time the Sadducees try to entrap Jesus by asking him about the resurrection and a woman married seven times. Here Jesus speaks of *the end*, the resurrection to eternal life after he comes again in glory, as another key for understanding God's plan for human love.

John Paul II puts his whole teaching in the framework of God's unfolding plan between these two reference points —"the beginning" and "the end" of human history.

He envisions this plan of salvation in four stages:

1. ORIGINAL HUMANITY (Paradise)
2. FALLEN HUMANITY
3. REDEEMED HUMANITY
4. GLORIFIED HUMANITY (Paradise again)

The first and last stages are completely beyond the boundaries of our experience. The only way we can possibly understand or imagine them is through God's authoritative word in the Bible. The second and third stages together are history as we know it, fallen and redeemed humanity, which overlap or coexist in our experience.

We can view the stages in a schema like this:

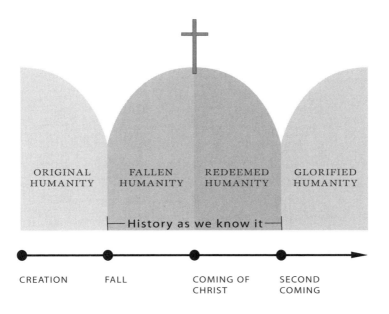

Chapters 2 through 5 in this study guide will focus on these four stages in turn. Here I will highlight some foundational principles of the theology of the body.

"MALE AND FEMALE HE MADE THEM"

As noted above, Jesus solemnly declares that marriage is indissoluble (unbreakable), and to justify that statement he refers to the intention of the Creator from the beginning. He thereby indicates that *the significance of marriage as a lifelong union is something inscribed in our very nature as God created us*. So John Paul II makes it his aim to reflect very deeply about what Scripture teaches us about "the beginning." And he finds, as most biblical scholars do, an immense density, depth and precision in those few short chapters about the beginning, Genesis 1–3.

The first thing the pope notes, as anyone who carefully reads Genesis sees, is that there are two different accounts of the creation of human beings. The first is in Genesis 1, where God creates man on the sixth day as part of the seven-day series:

> Then God said, "Let us make man [adam] in our image, after our likeness; and let them have dominion over the fish of the sea, and over the birds of the air, and over the cattle, and over all the earth, and over every creeping thing that creeps upon the earth." So God created man [adam] in his own image, in the image of God he created him; male and female he created them.[1]
>
> —GENESIS 1:26–27

The second account, in Genesis 2, describes man being made from the dust of the earth, then naming the animals. Then God forms the woman from the man's rib. This second account actually comes from an older tradition. Scholars call it the Yahwist account because in it God is called *Yahweh Elohim*, "the LORD God," whereas in Genesis 1 he is called just *Elohim*, "God."

The main point of the first account is that man, as male and female, is in the image of God. That is, human beings have a special relationship to God unlike that of any other creature. It is true that man is an animal, similar in some ways to the other animals, and yet there is something that sets him apart and reflects our divine Creator. Only the human being is a **person**. "And behold, it was *very* good," Scripture says after the creation of man (Genesis 1:31, emphasis added).

What is it about us that shows we are in the image of God? The traditional answer is our reason and free will. The pope affirms this answer, using the terms "self-awareness" (or "self-consciousness") and "self-determination."

Self-awareness (reason) is apparent by the fact that Adam *knows* the other animals, names them and recognizes himself as different from them. He is aware of himself as a "someone," not a "something."

We see Adam's self-determination in the fact that he can *freely choose*. Unlike the animals, he is given a commandment so as to be able to exercise his freedom: "Of the tree of the knowledge of good and evil you shall not eat" (Genesis 2:17). Only a human being is master of his own actions. Only a human being can know the truth and freely act in accord with it.

But John Paul II does not simply restate the traditional answer. Here is where he brings in one of his most profound insights. Genesis 1, he points out, does not say that God created us in his image as generic human beings but *as male and female*. Amazingly enough, in three thousand years no one had really grasped the significance of this line. It means that our very embodiment as either male or female—that is, our sexual complementarity—reveals something significant about us, and thus about God.

THE BODY MATTERS

In order to grasp the importance of this insight, we first have to reject some common misconceptions about the body. We all absorb certain attitudes about the body from the world around us. Our own culture's tendency is to idolize the human body and, at the same time, to demean it. For example, any advertisement not based on exploiting the body for its sex appeal is likely to be based on indulging the body, whether through sumptuous foods, hormone treatments or thrilling experiences.

Both these tendencies stem from a view of the body as insignificant; literally, it doesn't *signify* anything. What we do with the body, modern culture tells us, is inconsequential. Even some Christians tend to think of the body as a kind of afterthought or a mere shell to house the soul.

But for the Bible, the body has incalculable significance. The body is not just a part of the person; it *is* the person insofar as the person belongs to the physical world. We are not souls that happen to be attached to bodies; rather, we are *body persons*.

Even our language instinctively recognizes this truth. You are not likely to hear a child say to another, "Stop hitting my body!" but, "Stop hitting *me*!" We do not say, "Sue's body has cancer," but, "*Sue* has cancer." Can you imagine ever saying to someone, "I like you and want a relationship with you, but I don't want to see, hear, touch, smell or have any contact with your body"? What kind of a relationship would that be?

None at all, since the body is the very means by which we are present to the world and relate to one another.

The body, then, is the visible expression of the person. Or as the Pope puts it, the body is the *sacrament* of the person. He uses the word *sacrament* here in the broad sense, to mean "a visible sign of an invisible reality." The body is the outward sign that reveals the inner person.

MADE FOR UNION

What does the human body reveal? Considering the body, we can immediately recognize a profound truth: The male body has a marvelous and unique capacity for union with the female body, and the female body with the male. Evidently they were made to go together. Along with this capacity is a built-in desire for such a union, an attraction to and fascination with the opposite sex. *The body, in its sexual complementarity, reveals that we are created for relationship, for interpersonal union.*

Scripture expresses this truth through the words Adam spoke upon seeing Eve, his bride, for the first time: "This at last is bone of my bones and flesh of my flesh" (Genesis 2:23). Adam was thrilled! He recognized in Eve—unlike the animals—an equal, a person like himself whom he could *love*. That is, he saw someone to whom he could give himself completely and who could receive and reciprocate his gift to form a union that would fulfill the very meaning of their existence.

The Bible indicates that this deeply personal union, in which the man and woman become a gift to one another, is enacted in their bodies through the sexual embrace. "Therefore a man leaves his father and his mother and cleaves to his wife, and they become one flesh" (Genesis 2:24, the verse specifically cited by Jesus in Matthew 19:5). It is a union so real and profound that, with God's help, it can even take concrete form in the existence of another person.

Once we reflect on it, we find that the truth is evident: The body is made for spousal union. It is written in us, stamped in our sexual differentiation as male and female. God did not tell Adam and Eve to have a platonic relationship, to come to a meeting of minds, to be spiritually in sync. He told them to "be fruitful and multiply" (Genesis 1:28). They were to come together in a physical union that would signify and enact a personal union on the deepest level of their being.

We have to go back to the beginning, then, to listen to the message of the body that is inscribed in every person: I am capable of, and made for, a **communion of persons**—that is, an interpersonal union in which I freely give myself to another in love and receive love in return. The human body says, "I am a gift. I am capable of giving myself freely to another person in an intimate union of love." An animal body does not say this. A penguin, a baboon or an alligator can mate, but it cannot make a gift of self to another in an intimate union of love.

So how does this relate to our being in the image of God? Genesis gives us a hint, which will only be fully unveiled in the New Testament: "Let *us* make man…" (Genesis 1:26, emphasis added). That is, *God himself is a communion of Persons*, a Trinity in which the Father, Son and Holy Spirit pour themselves out in an eternal exchange of self-giving love. "God *is* love," proclaims Saint John (1 John 4:8, emphasis added). The Father gives himself completely to the Son, holding nothing back; the Son returns this gift in infinite love and gratitude. So real and life-giving is their communion that it eternally springs forth in the third Person of the Trinity, the Holy Spirit.

Genesis 1–2 thus reveals the immense significance of the body in God's plan. As John Paul II says,

> The body, and it alone, is capable of making visible what is invisible: the spiritual and the divine. It was created to transfer into the visible reality of the world the mystery hidden since time immemorial in God.[2]

The human body is capable of revealing God. This is why the Pope calls his reflections "the theology of the body." God is neither male nor female, because he is pure spirit. Yet the invisible mystery of Trinitarian love is imaged, or made visible, in our bodies when we form a communion of persons in truth and love.

A TRUTH AVAILABLE TO ALL

The fact that we are persons in the image of God gives us an inestimable dignity. One does not have to be a Christian to recognize this dignity. John Paul II has also written about human dignity from the perspective of philosophy. We all intuit that there is a unique value and worth in every person, which is not found in any other kind of being. Even the German philosopher Immanuel Kant, who was no devout Christian, formulated this principle: A human being is the only being that is an end in itself and can never be used as a means to an end.

John Paul II's particular brand of philosophy is called **phenomenological personalism**. This school of thought seeks to discover truths about reality by reflecting on experience.

For example, if you ask anyone, "Do you want to be loved or used?" who in his right mind would not choose love? We can all relate to the experience of wanting to be loved, not used, and of the profound suffering that occurs when we are used.

The human body says, "I am a person, and therefore I am of infinite value. I am to be treated with dignity and respect. The only proper response to me is love." All human beings are capable of recognizing this dignity if they read the truth imprinted in the human body.

Michelangelo's fresco on the ceiling of the Sistine Chapel depicts the human body as a visible reflection of our divine Creator.

STUDY TOOLS

Scriptures
Matthew 19:3–8
Genesis 1:26–27

Church Teaching
Man, who is the only creature on earth which God willed for himself, cannot fully find himself except through a sincere gift of self (Vatican II, *Gaudium et spes*, 24).

General Audiences of John Paul II
September 5 to November 14, 1979.

Key Concepts
Communion of persons: the kind of intimate union that can only exist between persons, through a sincere and mutual gift of self.

Person: a being with the capacity to know and to act freely, who is called to communion with other persons through a sincere gift of self.

Phenomenological personalism: *Phenomenology* is a philosophical method that is experience-oriented—that is, it begins with observing how things in the world present themselves to us rather than with a preformed system or categories. *Personalism* is a philosophy that begins with the all-important question "What is a person?" and the radical uniqueness of persons as distinct from every other kind of being. The philosophy of Pope John Paul II unites both these approaches, along with insights from Saint Thomas Aquinas.

Theology of the body: John Paul II's reflections on the meaning of the human person, love, sex and marriage in light of the body, as given in his general audiences from 1979 to 1984. These reflections, rooted in Scripture, recognize the fact that we do not just have bodies but *are* body persons, whose inner life is expressed through the body.

Questions for Reflection and Discussion
1. In your own words, explain why in Matthew 19 Jesus goes back to "the beginning" to teach us why marriage is indissoluble.

2. What are some examples of ways our contemporary culture both idolizes and demeans the body?

3. Read Genesis 1:26–31; 2:7 and 1 Corinthians 6:19–20. Have you ever thought about the fact that your body makes visible the invisible mystery of God? What changes does that call for in your attitude toward your body?

4. Read John 3:34–35; 14:31; 15:9. What do these verses teach you about God as a communion of persons? In what ways can your marriage or other relationships be a reflection of the love of the Trinity?

5. Can you relate to the experience of feeling used rather than loved? Conversely, can you relate to the experience of being loved and treated with proper human dignity? What do these experiences teach you about your responsibility toward other persons?

Practical Application

This week be alert to what you read, see or hear in the media and in ordinary conversation about the human body. Each time the topic comes up, ask the Lord to show you *his* perspective and to give you a greater reverence for the body as the visible expression of the person. Also pray this way each time you look in the mirror.

Memory Verse

God created man in his own image,
in the image of God he created him;
male and female he created them.

—GENESIS 1:27

Chapter Two

ORIGINAL HUMANITY

All the talk in Genesis about animals, a rib, a garden, a tree and a serpent may sound to us like a primitive fairy tale, not worthy of our serious attention. But this deceptively simple story hides unexpected depths of insight. As we saw in the previous chapter, the story of creation reveals truths about both God's original intention for human life and the primordial events that underlie human experience to this day.

The creation story is indeed "mythic"—not in the sense that it is fictional but in that it uses symbolic language to reveal profound truths about God and about the human condition. The ancient authors of Genesis were master psychologists as well as brilliant theologians. While the narrative refers to a real event at the dawn of human history, it contains much more than a purely literal account could convey.[1]

Only through what Scripture tells us about the beginning can we know what human life was meant to be, since our own experience is marked by sin and its consequences. The point of returning to the beginning is not only to rediscover the meaning of marriage but also to help us grasp the significance of being male and female. If marriage is an unbreakable union of love between a man and a woman, what kind of persons must we be to be capable of such a union?

The pope draws out three important aspects of life before the Fall as revealed in the Bible. These he calls **original solitude**, **original unity** and **original nakedness**.

NOT GOOD TO BE ALONE

Let us look more closely at the second creation account (Genesis 2), which depicts the creation of man and woman separately. First the man is fashioned from the dust of the earth, and God breathes into his nostrils the breath of life. Before Eve comes on the scene, God lets Adam (who represents all humanity) experience the fact that he is different from the rest of creation.

> Then the Lord God said, "It is not good that the man should be alone; I will make him a helper fit for him." So out of the ground the Lord God formed every beast of the field and every bird of the air, and brought them to the man to see what he would call them; and whatever the man called every living creature, that was its name. The man gave names to all cattle, and to the birds of the air, and to every beast of the field; but for the man there was not found a helper fit for him.
>
> —GENESIS 2:18–20

In a certain way Adam is alone before God. As he encounters the animals, he is aware that he is unique, utterly distinct from everything else in the visible world. He is not a "something" but a "someone," with the capacity to know and love and thus to interact with God. As John Paul II points out, this is true of every human being: I am aware of being a self, a *person* who transcends the rest of creation and is capable of relating to the Creator. The pope calls this experience "original solitude."

Adam discovered his uniqueness through his body. By encountering other living creatures, he became aware that only his body was the body of a person. This is true for us as well. Think of the way a child comes to understand herself as a self by recognizing other persons and objects around her. The body is the basis of both our awareness of ourselves and our relationships to others, including God.

The man in Genesis was aware that his existence was a gift from God, and that therefore he was called freely to enter into a relationship with God—to respond to him in love and gratitude. Adam, like every human being since, is called to an interior life; he is capable of hearing God and responding.

But the Bible also indicates that more was needed: "It is not good for the man to be alone." In his solitude Adam experienced a longing for another human person like himself—a "helper fit for him." We, too, are fulfilled only in communion with other human beings.

We should note that *helper* in this verse (*ezer* in Hebrew) does *not* mean "cook, laundress and scullery-maid." After all, it is God who is most often called our "helper" in the Old Testament (see, for instance, Exodus 18:4; Psalm 33:20). Rather, the helper the man needs is someone who can remind him of and help him to fulfill the deepest purpose of his life: that is, to *love*. In other words, the man needs the woman in order to be fully human, just as the woman needs the man.

THE TWO BECOME ONE

In response to Adam's longing, God does what he had planned all along: He causes the man to fall into a deep sleep and creates a woman from his rib—showing how closely she is related to him. Like the father of the bride, God presents Adam with his masterpiece. The man responds by crying out in a hymn of joy, expressing his happiness that he has encountered the body of another *person*—a body like his own, yet wonderfully different.

> Then the man said, "This at last is bone of my bones and flesh of my flesh; she shall be called Woman, because she was taken out of Man."
>
> —GENESIS 2:23

Adam recognizes that Eve shares his human nature, yet it is embodied in a different way. This sexual complementarity of the man and woman—their bodily differences within a common nature—reveals their call to relationship. In fact, their sexual differentiation is what enables them to become a mutual gift of self to one another. Their bodies' natural aptitude for union is the visible reflection of their interior capacity to form a communion of persons.

The care with which God carries out his design for humanity shows us that sexual differences are not just skin-deep. Sexuality is more than a superficial, biological attribute. It is not manipulatable like hair or eye color. Even the various methods that attempt to manipulate it surgically or pharmaceutically only change its exterior characteristics. Sexuality is integral to us as male or female persons.

The passage goes on: "Therefore a man leaves his father and his mother and cleaves to his wife, and they become one flesh" (Genesis 2:24). The husband and wife enact their "original unity" in sexual union, which expresses exteriorly what is true in their minds and hearts.

Here is where we find the insight that is the linchpin of the theology of the body: what the Pope calls the **nuptial meaning of the body**. The word *nuptial* calls to mind a wedding; it is synonymous with "spousal." *The nuptial meaning of the body is our call to self-giving love, which is written into our* *very embodiment as male or female.* By becoming a gift to one another in a communion of persons, *we learn to love and be loved as God loves*, and so fulfill our highest destiny. We become a reflection of the very life and love of the Trinity and prepare to share in that life forever. This is true for every human person, whether married, single or a consecrated celibate, though it is lived out in different ways.

The fullest expression of the nuptial meaning of the body, on a natural level, is marriage. The communion that exists in marriage is unique, in that the gift of self is total and exclusive. Its bodily expression is the sign of an unbreakable covenant bond, in which the spouses commit themselves to one another in a lifelong union. Only such a total gift of self is capable of authentic sexual expression.

God has also designed the love of spouses to be inherently expansive. The one-flesh union of husband and wife becomes "incarnate" in a mysterious way when a new human being is brought into the world. Thus their communion is widened to encompass new persons equal in dignity and equally worthy of unconditional acceptance, enabling the spouses to reflect even more fully the mystery of God's own love.

Human freedom finds its deepest realization in the marriage covenant. The world tells us that freedom means avoiding all commitment, but the truth is the opposite! True freedom is the ability to unite your whole being in choosing what is good, without any constraint. Who is more free: we who struggle with temptation or the saints in heaven, who have been so perfected in love that they cannot choose evil and can give themselves totally and unreservedly to God?

In fact, the covenant bond expressed in wedding vows is precisely for the purpose of freedom. Rather than remaining indefinitely open to a potential relationship with another person, I choose this one person to give myself to completely in an irrevocable union. I voluntarily channel all my freedom into a total gift of self to my chosen spouse—and through that person, to God. The covenant bond is the *fulfillment* of human freedom.

Although marriage is unique, it is not the only way of living out the nuptial meaning of the body. We are all called to become a gift of self to others through our God-given masculinity or femininity. We are all in need of "helpers"— whether parents, relatives, friends or coworkers—who can help us discover our call to self-giving love. Whenever we make a sincere gift of self to others through bodily actions showing love and respect, and that gift is affirmed and reciprocated, a communion of persons is formed. There is also a supernatural way of living out the nuptial meaning of the body, consecrated celibacy, which we will discuss in Chapter 5.

What about homosexual persons? For those who experience same-sex attraction, the truth about the human person revealed in our bodies is both challenging and liberating—as it is for everyone. Despite what the media often present, no one is "born homosexual." That is, no one is intrinsically oriented to union with the same sex.[2] Thus homosexual attraction does not define anyone in the essence of his or her identity.

In fact, properly speaking, *sexual* union is not possible with a person of the same sex. The fact that life-giving genital union is possible only with a person of the opposite sex is a visible sign that our call to spousal communion is through our innate complementarity as man and woman. The many severe health risks associated with homosexual activity also underscore the fact that such an orientation is not in accord with God's design.

This is not to imply that homosexual inclinations are in themselves sinful. They are but one form of the disorder in our desires that results from the Fall. Sin occurs only when we *act* on these fallen desires.

Where there is disorder and sin, there is also hope for restoration. By God's grace we can experience a healing of our identity as men and women in the image of God, as we will see in Chapter 4.

NAKED AND UNASHAMED

The second creation account concludes with this cryptic observation: "And the man and his wife were both naked, and were not ashamed" (Genesis 2:25). This nakedness without shame, John Paul II explains, means that before the Fall the first couple experienced unveiled communication with one another. They saw each other as God sees. Their bodies were transparent windows to the inner person. There was no danger of looking at the body as an object, separate from the person. Between the man and woman there was a depth of intimacy, communication and mutual understanding that we can hardly begin to imagine.

Adam and Eve expressed their reciprocal self-giving through their naked bodies. Through their femininity and masculinity, each became a total, faithful and potentially fruitful gift for the other. Through their one-flesh union they also came to a deeper self-understanding. This is why the Bible uses the expression "to know" for the marital embrace: "Now Adam knew Eve his wife, and she conceived" (Genesis 4:1).

The mention of nakedness without shame contrasts with the experience of shame after the Fall (see Genesis 3:7), which we will consider in Chapter 3. It points to a time when there was wholeness within human persons, when there was no rupture between the spiritual and the physical and no opposition between male and female. Imagine a world untouched by shame in all of our vulnerability to others, and you have a glimmer of our original created state.

This return to the beginning is not an abstract academic exercise. We can only know the full reality of who we are by "remembering" the beginning with the help of Scripture. It is here we can begin to understand our dignity as children of God and our destiny in the communion of love that is the Trinity.

Here, too, we come to understand that our bodies are integral to this dignity and destiny. Our bodies matter! They are not mere appendages to use, enjoy and discard, nor are they idols to be worshiped. They are the visible expression of our self-awareness and freedom, the means through which we grow and are perfected in love. Like the gospel message from which it is drawn, the theology of the body is good news that offers healing for us and our culture.

STUDY TOOLS
Scriptures
Genesis 1:26–28
Genesis 2

The original unity between man and woman, in which their bodies are a transparent expression of the inner person, is about to be disrupted by the father of lies.

Church Teaching

> The truth is that only in the mystery of the Incarnate Word does the mystery of man take on light. For Adam, the first man, was a figure of him who was to come, namely Christ the Lord. Christ, the final Adam, by the revelation of the mystery of the Father and his love, fully reveals man to himself and makes his supreme calling clear.
>
> —Vatican II, *Gaudium et spes*, 22

General Audiences of John Paul II
November 21, 1979, to April 2, 1980.

Key Concepts

Nuptial meaning of the body: the ability of the human body, in its masculinity or femininity, to express and realize our call to a communion of persons through self-giving love. Whether we are single, celibate or married, we discover through the body that the meaning of our existence is to be a gift.

Original nakedness: the condition of humanity before the Fall, in which the unclothed body did not cause shame. The body was a transparent expression of the person and therefore was not in danger of being treated as an object.

Original solitude: man's initial experience of being unique among created beings, capable of relating to God and others in self-awareness and freedom.

Original unity: the one-flesh union of the first married couple, based on their being equals who share the same human nature yet are sexually differentiated.

Questions for Reflection and Discussion

1. Prayerfully read Genesis 1—2, and note several ways in which Scripture indicates that man is distinct from all other created beings.

2. Genesis 1:27 points out that male and female *together* are the image of God. What does this teach us about the way men and women should relate to one another?

3. Look through the Bible to find passages that talk about God as Creator (the Psalms are a good place to start). What do they express about God's character?

4. Reflect on Romans 12:1; 2 Corinthians 4:10; and 1 Timothy 2:8–10. What are some ways that your body can be an expression of your gift of self to God and to others?

5. Can you think of some examples of the idea that freedom means the avoidance of commitment? Why do people think this way? How would you express to them a different view?

Practical Application

This week ask the Lord to give you a deeper understanding and acceptance of your identity as a man or woman. Then look for ways in which you can become a gift of self to those around you through gestures of love, affirmation, generosity and service.

Memory Verse

Therefore a man leaves his father and his mother and cleaves to his wife, and they become one flesh. And the man and his wife were both naked, and were not ashamed.

—GENESIS 2:24–25

Chapter Three

FALLEN HUMANITY

In the last chapter we considered the first stage in the span of human history: man and woman before the Fall. In that original state, humanity as created by God was pure, innocent, happy and unencumbered by sin and all its harmful consequences. Adam and Eve were joined in a blissful union of open communication and selfless reciprocal love. They experienced the fullness for which every married couple longs.

Why, we might ask, did God put all this beauty and freedom at risk by giving Adam and Eve a commandment that he knew they might break? Why did he put in the garden a tree from which he did not want them to eat?

The answer to these questions can be found by recalling God's intention from the beginning. God created the man and woman with a capacity to be united with him in love forever. Yet this capacity could not be fulfilled apart from their free choice. There is no such thing as love without freedom. By giving them the commandment (Genesis 2:16–17), God invited them to respond to him freely in love, trust and obedience—to let him be their God. He placed the tree of the knowledge of good and evil right in the middle of the garden, where they would constantly be faced with The Choice.

But as we know, our first parents did not accept this loving invitation.

THE SIN

> Now the serpent was more subtle than any other wild crea-
> ture that the Lord God had made. He said to the woman, "Did
> God say, 'You shall not eat of any tree of the garden'?" And
> the woman said to the serpent, "We may eat of the fruit of the
> trees of the garden; but God said, 'You shall not eat of the fruit
> of the tree which is in the midst of the garden, neither shall
> you touch it, lest you die.'" But the serpent said to the woman,
> "You will not die. For God knows that when you eat of it your
> eyes will be opened, and you will be like God, knowing good
> and evil." So when the woman saw that the tree was good for
> food, and that it was a delight to the eyes, and that the tree
> was to be desired to make one wise, she took of its fruit and
> ate; and she also gave some to her husband, and he ate.
>
> —GENESIS 3:1–6

Tempted by the serpent, Adam and Eve took the bait. They
decided that rather than honor God, they would prefer to be
their own gods. Rather than trust in their loving Creator, they
decided to determine what was good and evil for themselves.
By their disobedience they inaugurated the painful history of
humanity's subjugation to sin and death. It is the stage of
humanity with which we are quite familiar!

The disobedience of the first couple was not merely a vio-
lation of rules. It was a personal act. Afterward God said to
the man, "Have *you* eaten of the tree of which *I* commanded
you not to eat?" (Genesis 3:11; emphasis added). The point
was not that they ate from the wrong tree but that they dis-
trusted and disobeyed the Author of their lives.

Genesis conveys the magnitude of this **original sin**,
which affected all subsequent humanity, by describing Adam
and Eve's ejection from Paradise, the anguish of "labor" in

work and in childbirth, and the most tragic and inevitable consequence of all: death (see Genesis 3:9-24). In comparison with original humanity, our condition since the Fall is greatly diminished. But as we will see in the next chapter, since Christ has come, sin and death are not the last word for humanity. Without Christ man is fallen and unable to attain the destiny set for him by God. But with Christ humanity, while still wounded, is restored and full of promise.

The Fallout

As we saw in Chapter 2, God's plan for human beings was that we would experience union in the fullest sense. But the first sin caused *disunity*—not only between man and God but among human beings, between human beings and the created world, and even within the human being between spirit and body. Let us look at five specific effects of sin as described in Genesis.

1. Shame: Rupture within the Human Being

With original sin, as John Paul II observes, **concupiscence** enters the human heart. Concupiscence is a disorder in our desires that inclines us toward sin. Have you noticed how easily our desires can go awry? Even desires that are good in themselves, whether for food, comfort, rest, sexual pleasure or material goods, so easily gravitate toward imbalance and excess. Who cannot identify with the groan of Saint Paul, "I can will what is right, but I cannot do it. For I do not do the good I want, but the evil I do not want is what I do" (Romans 7:18–19)?

Concupiscence infects our sexuality in a singular way. Instead of seeing the body as a transparent expression of the inner life and true depth of the person, we are tempted to view the body as an object to be used for pleasure or self-gratification. The nuptial meaning of the body is veiled, and the very capacity to reveal and understand ourselves as gift is diminished. As a result, the body is vulnerable to exploitation.

The human heart has now become a battlefield between love and **lust**.[1] Instead of becoming a *gift*, we are tempted to *grasp*. Even married couples experience concupiscence: They are sometimes impelled by the desire to use and possess rather than to be a gift for one another. The Pope points out that whenever a man considers a woman to be only an object and not a gift, he at the same time condemns *himself* to become an object for her and not a gift.

"Then the eyes of both were opened, and they knew that they were naked; and they sewed fig leaves together and made themselves aprons" (Genesis 3:7). When Adam and Eve covered themselves with fig leaves and hid, the **shame** they experienced for the first time was a result of this rupture in the unity of spirit and body. This shame is deeper than mere embarrassment. It is a profound distress at the awareness of something contrary to their dignity as persons.

Shame, however, also has a positive purpose. Since the Fall, our inclination to cover certain parts of the body is a protection against the misuse of the body due to concupiscence. God himself covered the man and woman out of compassion: "The LORD God made for Adam and for his wife garments of skins, and clothed them" (Genesis 3:21).

In our fallen condition, when people deliberately expose (through scant clothing or tight clothing) those parts of the body that stimulate lust, they invite others to regard them as objects rather than persons. They undermine their own dignity as persons created in the image of God.

2. Fear: Rupture between Man and God

After their sin the man and woman no longer enjoy the free and unhindered fellowship with God they had before. Tormented by guilt, they now tend to fear God as a distant lawgiver and harsh judge.

> And they heard the sound of the LORD God walking in the garden in the cool of the day, and the man and his wife hid themselves from the presence of the LORD God among the trees of the garden. But the LORD God called to the man, and said to him, "Where are you?" And he said, "I heard the sound of [you] in the garden, and I was afraid, because I was naked; and I hid myself." He said, "Who told you that you were naked? Have you eaten of the tree of which I commanded you not to eat?"[2]
>
> —GENESIS 3:8–11

Humanity has been hiding from God ever since, though God never hid from man. He never ceases to call out to us, "Where are you?" Yet so often we try to avoid him in our guilt and fear. At the same time, we secretly long for the intimacy of the garden, where Adam and Eve walked in close familiarity with their Creator.

3. Conflict: Rupture in Human Relationships

The fellowship the first couple enjoyed with one another is also broken by sin. When God questions Adam, he replies by quickly pointing the finger at his wife.

> The man said, "The woman whom [you gave] to be with me, she gave me fruit of the tree, and I ate." Then the LORD God said to the woman, "What is this that you have done?" The woman said, "The serpent beguiled me, and I ate."[3]
>
> —GENESIS 3:12–13

Notice the contrast with the hymn of admiration Adam had uttered earlier (see Genesis 2:23). The man now distances himself from his wife and casts blame on her. The loving communion between the two has been torn, and from now on they have difficulty understanding and trusting one another.

God tells the woman: "Your desire shall be for your husband, and he shall rule over you" (Genesis 3:16). God is not expressing his own decree—much less his will—but rather an intrinsic consequence of sin. The relationship between man and woman has become warped. Whereas their sexual complementarity was meant to lead to a life-giving union, it now can tend toward tension and conflict. An adversarial stance develops between the two, which frequently plays out as domination on the part of the man and manipulation on the part of the woman. Man and woman cannot be human without each other, yet each is tempted to selfishly strive for self-promotion and self-protection to the detriment of the other.

Because the relation between man and woman, husband and wife, is the paradigm of all human relating, its degree of integrity or disintegration affects all of human life and all social relationships. In his letter *On the Dignity of Women*, John Paul II describes the effects of this disruption particularly upon the woman:

> Therefore when we read in the biblical description the words addressed to the woman: *"Your desire shall be for your husband, and he shall rule over you"* (Gn 3:16), we discover a break and a constant threat precisely in regard to this "unity of the two" which corresponds to the dignity of the image and likeness of God in both of them. But this threat is more serious for the woman.... This "domination" indicates the disturbance and *loss of the stability* of that *fundamental equality* which the man and the woman pos-

sess in the "unity of the two": and this is especially to the disadvantage of the woman.... [But] at the same time it also diminishes the true dignity of the man.[4]

4. Labor: Rupture between Man and the Created World

God also indicates to Adam and Eve that an intrinsic conse-quence of their sin is a disharmony within the whole created universe (see Romans 8:20–21).

> To the woman he said, "I will greatly multiply your pain in childbearing; in pain you shall bring forth children, yet your desire shall be for your husband, and he shall rule over you." And to Adam he said, "Because you have listened to the voice of your wife, and have eaten of the tree of which I commanded you, 'You shall not eat of it,' cursed is the ground because of you; in toil you shall eat of it all the days of your life."
> —GENESIS 3:16–17

Both men and women are now subject to "labor," each in his or her own way. The woman is promised labor in bringing forth children; her glory now also becomes her pain. Through man the earth is cursed and becomes recalcitrant, bringing forth produce only with difficulty. There is now a discord between humanity and the natural world, for which human-ity was supposed to care as God's royal representative (see Genesis 1:28). Man's efforts to fulfill the commission given to him by God, to have dominion over the earth, now become a strenuous exertion. It is significant, however, that the man and woman are not themselves cursed.

5. Death

The culmination of all these forms of disunity is death. Ultimately sin not only leads to death but *is* death—that is, it is the separation from God of which physical disintegration is only the outward sign (see Ephesians 2:1). "In the sweat of your face you shall eat bread till you return to the ground, for out of it you were taken; you are dust, and to dust you shall return" (Genesis 3:19).

In the Hebrew mind-set death is where there is no praise of God, because a person is cut off from communion with the Author of Life (see Psalm 115:17). In this perspective God's banishing Adam and Eve from the garden was actually an act of kindness. He did not want them to live forever physically in a condition of separation from him—a living death that would have been hell on earth.

> Then the Lord God said, "Behold, the man has become like one of us, knowing good and evil; and now, lest he put forth his hand and take also of the tree of life, and eat, and live for ever" —therefore the Lord God sent him forth from the garden of Eden, to till the ground from which he was taken. He drove out the man; and at the east of the garden of Eden he placed the cherubim, and a flaming sword which turned every way, to guard the way to the tree of life.
>
> —GENESIS 3:22–24

Despite all the destructive results of sin, Scripture never indicates that the Fall left man in a state of utter depravity. The image of God in man, though disfigured, was never lost. Even though the mind has become clouded by sin, human beings retain their natural ability to know God through his creation and to live according to their consciences (see Romans 1:19–20; 2:14). As male and female, we are still able to image God, to form a communion of persons with one another and to pass on human life, which is itself in the image of God. Our life is still a precious gift containing many blessings.

THE PROMISE

God's most severe pronouncement after the Fall is not to the man or woman but to the serpent who tempted them: "I will put enmity between you and the woman, and between your seed and her seed; he shall bruise your head, and you shall bruise his heel" (Genesis 3:15).

This declaration foretells a perpetual conflict between the serpent (Satan) and the woman and her descendant, on whom the serpent will inflict a blow. At the same time it is the first hint of a future salvation: The serpent will in turn be dealt a mortal blow (to the head) and so be vanquished in the end.

Through the whole poignant narrative of Genesis 3, God's inextinguishable mercy hovers in the background like a glimmer of sunrise to come. The promise of a descendant who would crush the head of the serpent is an intimation that God means to somehow reverse this terrible setback, and that his plans to glorify humanity have not been foiled permanently.

In the Christian perspective, even the story of the Fall is good news. It provides the true explanation for all our problems and thus keeps us from denial, false human optimism and counterfeit solutions. It is good news also because God did not leave us without the promise of restoration. The beautiful words of the *Exsultet,* sung at the Easter Vigil liturgy, remind us of how God works good even out of evil:

> What good would life have been to us,
> had Christ not come as our Redeemer?
> Father, how wonderful your care for us!
> How boundless your merciful love!
> To ransom a slave you gave away your Son.
> O happy fault, O necessary sin of Adam,
> which gained for us so great a Redeemer![5]

The man and woman are expelled from paradise on earth, but only after God has given them hope by promising a future restoration.

STUDY TOOLS

Scriptures
Genesis 3
Romans 3:9–24

Church Teaching

Man, tempted by the devil, let his trust in his Creator die in his heart and, abusing his freedom, disobeyed God's command. This is what man's first sin consisted of. All subsequent sin would be disobedience toward God and lack of trust in his goodness. In that sin man *preferred* himself to God and by that very act scorned him. He chose himself over and against God, against the requirements of his creaturely status and therefore against his own good. Created in a state of holiness, man was destined to be fully "divinized" by God in glory. Seduced by the devil, he wanted to "be like God," but "without God, before God, and not in accordance with God." (*CCC*, #397–98)

General Audiences of John Paul II
April 16 to October 29, 1980.

Key Concepts
Concupiscence: a disorder in our desires that inclines us toward sin. The *Catechism* states that "concupiscence stems from the disobedience of the first sin. It unsettles man's moral faculties and, without being in itself an offense, inclines man to commit sins" (*CCC, #* 2515).

Lust: indulging one's sexual desires while treating oneself or someone else as an object rather than a person.

Original sin: the sin by which our first parents disobeyed God's commandment, choosing to follow their own will instead of God's will. All human beings inherit the resultant fallen state and loss of original holiness.

Shame: the distress and tension created by treating another person, or being treated, as a mere object for use rather than as a gift to be honored and loved. Shame can also have the positive function of protecting the body from being so treated.

Questions for Reflection and Discussion
1. Prayerfully read Genesis 3, and write down all the instances in which you can see God's love and compassion for man and woman at work in the midst of this tragedy.

2. In what sense does all sin contain the same elements as the original sin—namely, distrust of God and disobedience?

3. Sin has resulted in a diminished existence. Does this mean that we are completely corrupt? What Old Testament verses can you find to support your answer? (Hint: Look at Psalm 8, Proverbs 31, Tobit 13.)

4. Do you ever subtly think, as Eve did, that God wants to deny you something good? What are some truths you could proclaim to yourself whenever you are tempted to think that way?

5. One of the effects of sin is fear. What does 1 John 4:18 teach you about this?

Practical Application

During the week examine your conscience as to how your own behavior toward your spouse or others close to you has been affected by the Fall. Choose one area in which to resolve to change by God's grace, and ask God for a healing of the ruptures caused by this sin.

Memory Verse

> Have mercy on me, O God,
> according to your steadfast love....
> For I know my transgressions,
> and my sin is ever before me...
> Create in me a clean heart, O God,
> and put a new and right spirit within me.
> Cast me not away from your presence,
> and take not [your] holy Spirit from me.
> Restore to me the joy of [your] salvation,
> and uphold me with a willing spirit.[6]
>
> —Psalm 51:1, 3, 10–12

Chapter Four

REDEEMED HUMANITY

The New Testament proclaims the fulfillment of God's promise to fallen humanity. Something entirely new and totally unexpected has happened: In Jesus the ancient curse of sin has been broken! Death has been destroyed, Satan has been conquered, and man has at last been reconciled to God. In other words, a new stage of human history—redeemed humanity—has begun.

John Paul II introduces this section of his catecheses with another unexpected Scripture passage. He grounds the entire section (twenty-seven general audiences) on Christ's words in Matthew 5:27–28: "You have heard that it was said, 'You shall not commit adultery.' But I say to you that everyone who looks at a woman lustfully has already committed adultery with her in his heart." He comes back to this saying of Christ in every address of this section, always on a deeper level and with new insights.

The pope likes to begin with the "hard sayings." These are the words of Jesus that many find offensive because they seem too idealistic, too rigorous and too severe. They are the words that many attempt to water down or reinterpret to accommodate our weakness. John Paul II does not bend the words of Christ at all, but with great skill he draws out their positive meaning, the beautiful vision of human possibilities that they actually reveal.

SLAVES OF LUST?

The pope notes that Jesus' statement may seem at first to be an accusation of the human heart: "Everyone who looks at a woman lustfully..." But the Lord's words "do not allow us to stop at the accusation of the human heart and to regard it continually with suspicion. They must be understood and interpreted above all as an *appeal to the heart.*"[1] Jesus is proclaiming that we are not condemned to live as prey to lust. He is calling us to rediscover the nuptial meaning of the body, and so to fulfill the deepest purpose of our lives.

The key is to recognize that Jesus does not just command us but *empowers* us. Suppose he said to a quadriplegic, "Stop slumping in that wheelchair." The quadriplegic might respond, "What do you mean? How can I do anything *but* slump in this wheelchair?" But Jesus' words are not like anyone else's. His very words have the power to enable the man to get up and walk. So Jesus' words to us about lust both signify and empower a whole new way of living, a way that goes back to God's original intention.

How is this possible? Through the grace of redemption, poured out in the act of love in which Jesus died for us on the cross.

"The words Christ uttered in the Sermon on the Mount are not a call hurled into emptiness."[2] They are efficacious words: They have power to accomplish what they call us to, if we listen to this interior call. Jesus did not come just to give us a stricter moral code. Is that the best the Son of God could do for us? No, he gave us the capacity to live out the true meaning of human existence, which is to participate in God's own love. We are no longer fallen humanity, ruled by lust. Because Christ came and died for us, we are redeemed humanity.

Often the message of contemporary culture is, in effect, "Slump! We cannot overcome our cravings for sex, or money or power. The best we can do is manipulate or restrain them." This message takes on various subtle forms. For example, instead of teaching teenagers the dignity of their bodies and a vision for sexuality, we say, "They're bundles of hormones. We can't really change their sex habits. Give them condoms." Instead of explaining to young adults the beauty of nuptial union when we see them living together outside marriage, we look the other way. This is a betrayal of the gospel and a plundering of the joy and fulfillment of God's plan.

In contrast, the Lord says, "Get up and walk!" So what does it mean to walk?

EROS AND ETHOS

The pope notes that Christ's words in Matthew 5:27–28 seem at first to be a severe warning against **eros** or erotic passion. Jesus seems to demand that sexual passion be crushed and destroyed. But this would be a false interpretation.

Eros is part of the interior force that attracts us to all that is good, true and beautiful. It is an echo of God, who is the supreme Goodness, Truth and Beauty. Eros is good; it is part of the way God created us! This includes the mutual attraction between the sexes, which is oriented toward the one-flesh union of husband and wife. God has written into us the gift of communion, the mysterious reality of his image. And he has built into us the desire that leads to the primary expression of that communion: marriage. Thus eros is not to be crushed but transformed.

How is eros transformed? By being united with **ethos**, true moral values or ethics.

We tend to think of ethics in negative terms: rules, commandments and prohibitions. But John Paul II shows that Jesus' words are not just a prohibition but rather express an essential *positive value* that they protect and liberate. Eros and ethos—passion and purity— "are not opposed to each other, but are called to meet in the human heart, and, in this meeting, to bear fruit."[3]

> It is necessary to rediscover continually in what is erotic the nuptial meaning of the body and the true dignity of the gift. This is the role of the human spirit, a role of an ethical nature. If it does not assume this role, the attraction of the senses and the passion of the body may stop at mere lust devoid of ethical value. Then man, male and female, does not experience that fullness of eros, which means the aspiration of the human spirit toward what is true, good and beautiful.[4]

The real problem is not eros but lust, which distorts and cheapens eros by reducing the other person to an object. In a sense the pope is saying that sexual desire that is mere lust is not erotic *enough!* It is a counterfeit of true eros. It sees only the surface and regards the body as a mere object for one's gratification. It fails to recognize the true dignity and preciousness of the human person revealed through the body.

John Paul II is in no way reducing the severity of Christ's words. He *is* saying that in Christ we now have the capacity to become the true masters of our own deep impulses, "like a guardian who watches over a hidden spring."[5] Particularly in the area of relations with the opposite sex, we have to rediscover the spiritual beauty of the human person revealed through the body in its masculinity and femininity. Christ has liberated the human heart, so that we are now able to sift out the gold of the nuptial meaning of the body from all the ugly accretions of lust.

If this high goal seems humanly unattainable, it is. But it *is* possible through life according to the Spirit.

Life in the Spirit

In his next section of teachings, John Paul II turns from Matthew to Paul, the great teacher of life in the Spirit. Paul's teaching is a faithful echo of Jesus' teaching in the Sermon on the Mount, helping us to understand how Christ's redemption can actually become a power at work in our lives. The key is the Holy Spirit, who gives us access to all that Jesus did in his death and resurrection. The Holy Spirit lovingly penetrates those areas of our personality that would hold us captive. He opens up the mysteries of God's love, sets us free and enables us to *experience* the new life we have in Christ.

John Paul II's starting point in this section of catecheses is Galatians 5:17: "The desires of the flesh are against the Spirit, and the desires of the Spirit are against the flesh." For Paul *flesh* does not mean our physical bodies. It means our disordered desires (concupiscence), which are enslaved by worldly values and which incline us toward sin. The works of the flesh include not only what we think of as "carnal" sins like extramarital sex, but also divisive evils like "idolatry, sorcery, enmity, strife, jealousy, anger, selfishness, dissension, party spirit, envy" (Galatians 5:20–21).

Galatians 5:17 describes the tension within us between fallen and redeemed humanity, between being ruled by the flesh and being ruled by the Spirit. We see this again in Romans 8:5–9:

> For those who live according to the flesh set their minds on the things of the flesh, but those who live according to the Spirit set their minds on the things of the Spirit. To set the mind on the flesh is death, but to set the mind on the Spirit is life and peace. For the mind that is set on the flesh is hostile to God; it does not submit to God's law, indeed it cannot; and those who are in the flesh cannot please God. But you are not in the flesh, you are in the Spirit, if in fact the Spirit of God dwells in you.

The Holy Spirit is a power at work in us, actively resisting the flesh and enabling us to take on instead the very life of Christ, a life of self-giving love. If we cooperate with him in this battle, setting our minds on the Spirit and letting the flesh be crucified, we will begin to experience the reality of redeemed humanity.

PASSION AND PURITY

John Paul II's teaching helps us to recognize the error of two false alternatives: promiscuity, in which distorted eros, or lust, is given free rein, and prudishness, in which eros is denied or repressed. Neither of these is true to our dignity as body persons in the image of God. The first views man as a mere animal; the second views man as a disembodied angel. Both are based on a devaluation of the body (a perennial human temptation, known in the ancient world as the heresy of **Manichaeism**).

The true answer for putting our sexuality in right order is **purity of heart**, to which Jesus calls us in the Sermon on the Mount: "Blessed are the pure in heart, for they shall see God" (Matthew 5:8). Purity is not a midway point between promiscuity and prudishness. It transcends both by liberating the nuptial meaning of the body. It enables us to channel our desires toward the true value of the person. There is no genuine love without purity.

Purity is a **virtue**, an aptitude that we acquire through consistent "abstention from unchastity." In this sense it demands a painful process of crucifying the flesh. But at the same time purity is a *gift* of the Holy Spirit, given only through redemption in Christ. Purity matures in the heart of the person who cultivates it, to the point that the person enjoys the fruits of the victory won over lust. Purity restores to the experience of the body—especially in the relations between man and woman—all its simplicity and its interior joy.[6] This joy is utterly different from the satisfaction of lust.

Purity includes the virtue of **temperance** or self-control, the mastery of one's desires (see Galatians 5:22–24). Undeniably, temperance can sometimes feel like emptiness and restriction, the very opposite of freedom—especially when it is attempted for the first time and if habits of lust have already been formed.[7] The pope is a realist. Temperance is not easy!

Yet temperance means *more*, not *less*. Gradually the temperate person begins to experience the **interior freedom of the gift**, the ability to experience the true meaning of life as self-gift in love and purity. The innermost layers of the person's human potential acquire a voice, layers that the lust of the flesh would hide.

Christian preaching can sometimes give the impression that morality is basically a series of no-no's: no casual sex, no homosexuality, no living together before marriage, no contraception, no pornography (basically, *no fun*, as the media portray it). Rather, we should thank God for Christian morality! It is not ultimately a "no" but a "yes." It is all about true freedom, about liberating the desires God has built into us for their full potential. The passion of lust (grasping for *me*) is transformed into the passion of gift (giving myself for *you*).

Think of the difference between a man who treats a woman as a sex object and a man who is passionately attracted to a woman but treats her with reverence and care, delighting in the beauty of her femininity and of the inner person revealed through her body. Passion united with purity frees the body to do what it was created to do: to be a living expression of the spiritual communion in which persons become a gift of self to one another.

> Purity is the glory of the human body before God. It is God's glory in the human body, through which masculinity and femininity are manifested. From purity springs that extraordinary beauty which permeates every sphere of men's common life and makes it possible to express in it simplicity and depth, cordiality and the unrepeatable authenticity of personal trust.[8]

John Paul II exemplified this purity, free from prudishness, in his own deep and lifelong friendships with women.

TEMPLE OF THE HOLY SPIRIT

Finally the pope notes that the human body has inestimable dignity not only because it expresses the human spirit, but even more, because of the indwelling presence of the Holy Spirit. Through Christ's uniting himself with humanity in his incarnation, death and resurrection, the human body has acquired a greater honor than it had even before the Fall. This new dignity brings a new obligation.

> Shun immorality. Every other sin which a man commits is outside the body; but the immoral man sins against his own body. Do you not know that your body is a temple of the Holy Spirit

within you, which you have from God? You are not your own;
you were bought with a price. So glorify God in your body.

—1 CORINTHIANS 6:18–20

If we live according to the true purpose of our lives, our
bodies become vehicles and expressions of God's own love.
The pope bears witness that human possibilities, human dignity, human love, are so much greater than the superficial
drone of the world would have us think.

This image of the Samaritan woman at the well (see John 4:1-30) beauti-
fully expresses the truth about redeemed humanity and the transformation of the relationship between men and women. The Samaritan
woman's life was out of order: She had five husbands and was living
with yet another man. Jesus, instead of rejecting her or prudishly stand-
ing aloof from her as was the custom ("they marveled that he was
talking to a woman"), invited her into a relationship with himself and
began to put her life in right order. He presented himself as the true
Bridegroom. He read her heart, and she knew she was loved.

STUDY TOOLS

Scriptures
Matthew 5:27–28
Romans 8:20–23
1 Corinthians 6:19–20
Galatians 5:16–23

Church Teaching
"By his Passion, Christ delivered us from Satan and from sin. He merited for us the new life in the Holy Spirit. His grace restores what sin had damaged in us" (*CCC,* # 1708).

General Audiences of John Paul II
November 5, 1980, to April 8, 1981.

Key Concepts
Eros: romantic or sexual desire for a person of the opposite sex. *Eros* is part of the God-given interior force that attracts us to all that is good, true and beautiful.

Ethos: that which corresponds to true moral or ethical values.

Interior freedom of the gift: the ability to give oneself to another in sincere love and purity, through self-mastery made possible by Christ's redemption.

Manichaeism: a dualistic philosophy that views the human body and everything belonging to the material realm as evil or worthless. Manichaeism sees only the spiritual realm as valuable.

Purity of heart: the freedom to see the body in its true dignity as an expression of the inner person, rather than as an object for the satisfaction of one's own desires. Purity is a virtue acquired by practicing temperance, but also a gift of the Holy Spirit.

Temperance: the virtue of self-control, which enables a person to master his desires rather than be mastered by them.

Virtue: a habitual and firm disposition to do what is good, brought about either by repeated action or by a gift of grace.

Questions for Reflection and Discussion

1. Reflect on Matthew 5:8, James 3:16–18 and Titus 1:15. In what ways does a pure person more truly "see" another person than an impure person can?

2. In your own words, explain how purity of heart is different from both promiscuity and prudishness.

3. How can an eros that is united to ethos be more passionate than a lustful eros?

4. Prayerfully read Romans 8:5–10 and Galatians 5:13–26. What are some ways in which the Lord is calling you to set your mind on the Spirit rather than the flesh?

5. In the past, what has been your interior reaction to Jesus' teaching in Matthew 5:26–27? Does the theology of the body bring about any different response in you to these words?

6. How might the Lord be calling you to "rediscover the nuptial meaning of your body"?

Practical Application

Think of someone you know who seems to have lost a sense of his or her dignity and worth as a person. Ask the Holy Spirit to show you a specific way that you can build up this person in love this week. Also ask for the gift of purity of heart in all your relationships.

Memory Verses

Walk by the Spirit, and do not gratify the desires of the flesh.

—GALATIANS 5:16

Do you not know that your body is a temple of the Holy Spirit within you, which you have from God? You are not your own; you were bought with a price. So glorify God in your body.

—1 CORINTHIANS 6:19–20

Chapter Five

GLORIFIED HUMANITY

Having traversed the first three stages in the panorama of human history, we come now to the final end that God has planned for us from all eternity: glorified humanity. The destiny for which we were created, and compared to which life on earth is a fleeting shadow, is to be bodily raised up and united in love with the holy Trinity forever. The splendor and surpassing joy of that end is beyond anything we can possibly imagine (see 1 Corinthians 2:9–10).

Christians live in the hope of this full accomplishment of God's work of salvation, yet we are meant to experience a foretaste of it even now, as we learn to give and receive love in accord with the nuptial meaning of our bodies. The trials and sufferings that are part of our growth in holiness are daily preparing us for this full accomplishment of God's work of salvation:

> For this slight momentary affliction is preparing for us an eternal weight of glory beyond all comparison, because we look not to the things that are seen but to the things that are unseen; for the things that are seen are transient, but the things that are unseen are eternal.
>
> —2 CORINTHIANS 4:17–18

Not only human beings but the whole cosmos longs for the transformation that will occur on that last day, when our bodies are raised from the dead (see Romans 8:19–21).

John Paul II begins this section of his teachings with the passage where the Sadducees present Jesus with a hypothetical question about the future life:

> And Sadducees came to him, who say that there is no resurrection; and they asked him a question, saying, "Teacher, Moses wrote for us that if a man's brother dies and leaves a wife, but leaves no child, the man must take the wife, and raise up children for his brother. There were seven brothers; the first took a wife, and when he died left no children; and the second took her, and died, leaving no children; and the third likewise; and the seven left no children. Last of all the woman also died. In the resurrection whose wife will she be? For the seven had her as wife." Jesus said to them, "Is not this why you are wrong, that you know neither the scriptures nor the power of God? For when they rise from the dead, they neither marry nor are given in marriage, but are like angels in heaven. And as for the dead being raised, have you not read in the book of Moses, in the passage about the bush, how God said to him, 'I am the God of Abraham, and the God of Isaac, and the God of Jacob'? He is not God of the dead, but of the living; you are quite wrong."
>
> —MARK 12:18–27

The real motive for the Sadducees' question is not genuine spiritual inquiry but an attempt to force Jesus into conceding that there is no such thing as a resurrection of the body. Their dilemma shows, however, that the Sadducees are ignorant of two things: the Scriptures and the power of God. Jesus addresses these two points in inverse order.

"The power of God" means God's power not only to restore man to life but to give him a completely new and transformed existence. As the Giver of Life, God is not bound by the law of death which rules our earthly history.

"The Scriptures," in this context, refers specifically to a passage in Exodus where God tells Moses, "I am the God of your father, the God of Abraham, the God of Isaac, and the God of Jacob" (Exodus 3:6). Jesus points out that for God to be the God *of someone,* that person must be in his presence and therefore alive! Even more, to be the "God of Abraham" means to be his protector and thus to keep him from death (in its most profound sense of being forever separated from God). And if it is *Abraham* who is kept from death, it must be the whole Abraham—that is, Abraham body and soul, as a body person.

By repeating, "You are wrong.... You are quite wrong," Jesus strongly emphasizes the importance of this truth of the resurrection of the body. Yet how many of us are barely aware of this truth, despite the fact that we recite it in the Creed every Sunday?

THE BODY IN THE LIFE TO COME

As with original humanity, we have knowledge of glorified humanity only through God's revealed Word. What will the resurrected life be like? Jesus indicates two significant facts in his answer to the Sadducees. First, by saying that "in the resurrection they neither marry [as men on earth do] nor are given in marriage [as women on earth are]," he indicates that in the risen life our bodies will still be male or female. The transformed life that God has prepared for us from all eternity is still a *human* life. Because we are body persons, our gender is a permanent dimension of our being, even in heaven.

At the same time, Jesus teaches us that in the future life maleness and femaleness will be different than on earth. Our sexual differentiation will no longer be connected with sexual union and procreation, but instead we will be "like angels." This does not mean that we will become disembodied spirits, but that we will have a heavenly and eternal existence like the angels, who have no need to reproduce. The nuptial meaning of the body will then be fully revealed "as the virginal meaning of being male and female."[1]

Our bodies will become the expression of a nuptial union with God himself that will infinitely transcend the earthly one-flesh union of husband and wife. In this heavenly marriage, the deepest meaning of the body will be fulfilled, as each person becomes a total gift of self in perfect communion with God and one another. Each person will be made immeasurably happy by union with the divine Bridegroom, yet this joy will increase as it is shared in the communion of saints.

Saint Paul further develops Jesus' teaching, based on Paul's own encounter with the risen Lord. Paul teaches us that our bodies will not only be restored to life but totally renewed (good news for those of us who are not entirely happy with our earthly bodies!). No longer will there be any sickness, pain or physical disintegration. The opposition between spirit and body with which we constantly struggle will end. The body will be spiritualized; that is, it will be permeated by and in perfect harmony with the Holy Spirit.

> So is it with the resurrection of the dead. What is sown is perishable, what is raised is imperishable. It is sown in dishonor, it is raised in glory. It is sown in weakness, it is raised in power. It is sown a physical body, it is raised a spiritual body.
> —1 CORINTHIANS 15:42–44

In heaven we will see God face-to-face and become like him (see 1 John 3:2). This is what the fathers of the church called *deification*. We will share in the inner life of the Trinity (see 2 Peter 1:4). This will not mean the disappearance of our own personal identity but rather its fullest realization.

What a vision of God's love for us the Bible portrays! We will be the joyful recipients of the personal gift of the Triune God in the very depths of our being. This is what we were created for.

> Participation in divine nature, participation in the interior life of God himself, penetration and permeation of what is essentially human by what is essentially divine, will then reach its peak so that the life of the human spirit will arrive at such fullness which previously had been absolutely inaccessible.[2]

Although this glory is yet to come, even now, by the work of the Holy Spirit, we can experience the first fruits of glorified humanity. As noted above, the whole purpose of our life on earth is to learn to love and be loved as God loves and so prepare to share in his life forever. With each decision we make to become a gift of self rather than to grasp for use and possession, we become more like Christ and live out more fully the nuptial meaning of the body.

The saints are our models in this process of deification. Observe how completely they yielded to God's gift of himself and how radically they responded in a reciprocal gift of self to God, whether in the vocation of marriage or of celibacy. As we follow their example, we, too, begin to move across the threshold and into the reality of eternal life—although not fully, until we enter into glory.

CELIBACY FOR THE KINGDOM

It is in the context of glorified humanity that John Paul II begins his reflections on the charism of **celibacy**. Only in the perspective of the heavenly marriage between God and his people can the celibate vocation be properly understood.

Before Jesus came, there was no such thing as a vocation to celibacy. The Jewish people saw marriage as the greatest blessing and fulfillment possible in human life, based on God's own word in Genesis 1:28. Indeed, it was considered a terrible misfortune and even a curse to die without having had a spouse or children (see Judges 11:37). So when Jesus spoke to his disciples about celibacy for the sake of the kingdom, he was instituting something radical and utterly new:

> For there are eunuchs who have been so from birth, and there are eunuchs who have been made eunuchs by men, and there are eunuchs who have made themselves eunuchs for the sake of the kingdom of heaven. He who is able to receive this, let him receive it.
>
> —MATTHEW 19:12

As John Paul II points out, by using the stark term *eunuch,* Jesus was alluding to the self-denial involved in embracing a call to celibacy. Jesus did not want to gloss over the fact that this vocation involves a renunciation.

At the same time Jesus indicates that celibacy for the kingdom is a *charism*, a gift that God bestows on whom he wills, inviting them to freely accept it. Paul also states this in 1 Corinthians 7:7. Those who receive this gift are so deeply moved by the love of Christ, the divine Bridegroom, that they desire to reciprocate it in a radical way. They do not reject their sexuality; rather they make a complete gift of their sexuality to God. To generously embrace this call is a source of joy and of abundant fruitfulness—of spiritual motherhood or fatherhood.

Like earthly marriage, consecration to Christ in a vow of lifelong celibacy is the expression of a total and exclusive gift of self. A celibate woman is spousally united to Christ, and a celibate man is spousally united to the church, in a way that is not compatible with spousal union with another person. There is total availability and total belonging.

A celibate person takes the deepest mystery of who he or she is, including sexuality, and gives it wholly and irrevocably to God. This vocation proclaims to others in the language of the body: "The love of God is real, and it is all-sufficient. You don't need sex and marriage in order to be fulfilled as a person."

COMPLEMENTARY VOCATIONS

Jesus' affirmation of this special calling is in no way a devaluation of marriage. On the contrary, the celibate vocation safeguards the fact that marriage, too, is a holy calling from the Lord, not a biological or emotional necessity. To renounce marriage for the sake of Christ has value precisely because marriage is good in itself.

At the same time, celibacy for the kingdom is a sign that marriage and procreation, good as they are, belong only to this life. There will be no marriage in heaven, because the heavenly wedding of which earthly marriage is a sign will infinitely surpass it. Those who have the charism of celibacy anticipate, in a certain way, that heavenly wedding now. They are symbols of the life to which we are all called for eternity. Thus it would be a mistake to view celibacy as something chosen merely to gain more time and efficiency in doing good works.

As Saint Paul explains, celibacy is for the sake of giving oneself wholly to God:

> I want you to be free from anxieties. The unmarried man is
> anxious about the affairs of the Lord, how to please the
> Lord; but the married man is anxious about worldly
> affairs, how to please his wife, and his interests are divided.
> And the unmarried woman or girl is anxious about the
> affairs of the Lord, how to be holy in body and spirit; but
> the married woman is anxious about worldly affairs, how
> to please her husband. I say this for your own benefit, not
> to lay any restraint upon you, but to promote good order
> and to secure your undivided devotion to the Lord.
>
> —1 CORINTHIANS 7:32–35

Such undivided adherence to the Lord is possible because of
the presence of the kingdom in Jesus Christ. By bringing us
into the family of God, Jesus has given us a new vision of
human life that relativizes the importance of the things of this
world—even of family ties with husband or wife, parents or
children (see Matthew 10:37). Because of *his* transformed
humanity present in our hearts by faith, it is possible to live
now in a way that already shares in the worship of the saints
and angels who see God (see Revelation 4–5). This special
vocation thus shows to all that "the form of this world is pass-
ing away" (1 Corinthians 7:31).

Just as two married people symbolize the relationship that
Christ has now to his church (and their commitment is a sacrament), so the celibate person is an icon of that relationship as
it will be perfected in heaven. The church needs both married
and celibate Christians. They are two complementary ways of
serving the Lord. Each vocation strengthens and elevates the
other when they are lived with integrity. Both married and celibate people are called to practice **chastity**, that is, the right
ordering of their sexuality within an inner unity of body and
spirit, which makes authentic self-giving love possible.

Tradition has maintained that the celibate way of life is the "better part" in that it more closely resembles the goal of our life (see 1 Corinthians 7:38). But subjectively, what is best for each individual is to embrace the vocation to which God has personally called him or her. "Each has his own special gift from God, one of one kind and one of another" (1 Corinthians 7:7). It is in living out our vocation with sincerity and perseverance that we grow in holiness and are made ready for "what no eye has seen, nor ear heard, nor the heart of man conceived, what God has prepared for those who love him" (1 Corinthians 2:9).

This image of the Transfiguration shows us Christ's human body radiant and suffused with his divine glory. His body is a sign and anticipation of what our glorified bodies will be like in heaven.

STUDY TOOLS

Scriptures
Matthew 22:23–33
Romans 8:19-21
1 Corinthians 15:35–53
1 John 3:2

Church Teaching

> In death, the separation of the soul from the body, the human body decays and the soul goes to meet God, while awaiting its reunion with its glorified body. God, in his almighty power, will definitively grant incorruptible life to our bodies by reuniting them with our souls, through the power of Jesus' Resurrection. (*CCC*, # 997)

General Audiences of John Paul II
November 11, 1981, to July 21, 1982.

Key Concepts
Celibacy for the kingdom: the voluntary renunciation of earthly marriage for the sake of spousal union with Christ (for a woman) or with the church (for a man).

Chastity: the right ordering of sexuality within an inner unity of body and spirit, which makes authentic self-giving love possible. This virtue is to be practiced by all Christians, whatever their state in life. For the unmarried, chastity entails abstinence from sex; for the married, chastity means that all sexual desires and behaviors are a sincere expression of the marriage covenant.

Questions for Reflection and Discussion

1. Read Matthew 22:30 and 1 Corinthians 15:35–53. What insights do these passages give you about our glorified bodies in heaven?

2. Prayerfully reflect on 1 Corinthians 7:29–31, Philippians 3:20–21 and 1 John 3:1–3. What are some specific ways that your attitude toward this life might change as hope for the resurrection of the body begins to fill your mind?

3. Reflect on 1 Corinthians 6:13–14. How does this passage help us understand Christian chastity?

4. Read 1 Corinthians 7:29–31. In your experience, what are some ways that the charism of celibacy and the sacrament of marriage complement each other in the church?

5. Meditate for a few minutes on the promises of God, his generosity, his respect for the human nature with which he has created us, and write a prayer of gratitude.

Practical Application

As often as possible think about heaven this week (avoiding clichés about clouds and harps). Ask the Lord to give you a sense of hope and excitement as you look forward to having your body glorified and being with him and your loved ones for all eternity.

Memory Verse

> I consider that the sufferings of this present time are not worth comparing with the glory that is to be revealed to us…. Creation itself will be set free from its bondage to decay and obtain the glorious liberty of the children of God.
>
> —ROMANS 8:18, 21

Chapter Six

MARRIAGE: THE PRIMORDIAL SACRAMENT

The more we read the Word of God, the more we discover the theme that pervades it: the theme of nuptial love. The first human words quoted in Scripture are those of a bridegroom: Adam's exclamation of wonder upon seeing Eve, his bride, for the first time. The very last words in Scripture are "The Spirit and the Bride say, Come!"—expressing the yearning of the church for Christ, her heavenly Bridegroom. In the middle of the Bible is the Song of Songs, the great mystical expression of the romance between God and his people. From Adam and Eve to the eternal wedding feast of the Lamb, God speaks of his love for us as the love of a husband for his bride.

Marriage is, in fact, the Bible's deepest underlying symbolic key for expressing the relationship between God and man. As the pope writes, "That mystery, as God's salvific plan in regard to humanity, is in a certain sense the central theme of all revelation, its central reality." This is why he calls marriage the "primordial" **sacrament**: It is "the most ancient revelation (manifestation) of the plan in the created world."[1]

Primordial here does not mean "greatest." The greatest sacrament is the Eucharist, the source and summit of the Christian life. Rather, *primordial* means "first in order" or "foundational." Even the Eucharist is "nuptial": Each time we celebrate it, it is a renewal of Christ's total self-gift to us on the cross and our response in love and gratitude as his bride. "[I]n a certain sense all the sacraments of the new covenant find their prototype in marriage as the primordial sacrament."[2]

For this section of his teaching the pope turns to Ephesians 5:21–33, the passage that most clearly draws the analogy between the union of spouses and the union of Christ with his church. Paul speaks of this analogy as a "great mystery." Let us first look at the biblical background of this passage.

ISRAEL, BRIDE OF GOD

The prophets of Israel developed in great depth the imagery of spousal love. For them this imagery was often in the context of a reproach. The chosen people did not understand nor reciprocate God's passionate love for them. Instead they responded with infidelity and betrayal, especially in the form of idolatry, the worship of alien gods. "Surely, as a faithless wife leaves her husband, so have you been faithless to me, O house of Israel, says the LORD" (Jeremiah 3:20).

Yet as inconstant as the people were, God again and again responded with patience and abiding compassion.

> For your Maker is your husband, the Lord of hosts is his name; and the Holy One of Israel is your Redeemer, the God of the whole earth he is called. For the Lord has called you like a wife forsaken and grieved in spirit, like a wife of youth when she is cast off, says your God. For a brief moment I forsook you, but with great compassion I will gather you.... For the mountains may depart and the hills be removed, but my steadfast love shall not depart from

you, and my covenant of peace shall not be removed, says the Lord, who has compassion on you.

—ISAIAH 54:5–7, 10

You shall no more be termed Forsaken, and your land shall no more be termed Desolate; but you shall be called My delight is in her, and your land Married; for the LORD delights in you, and your land shall be married. For as a young man marries a virgin, so shall your sons marry you, and as the bridegroom rejoices over the bride, so shall your God rejoice over you.

—ISAIAH 62:4–5

The pope observes, "These words brim over with the authentic ardor of love." They go "back to the mystery hidden in the heart of God."[3] They reveal that God's love for his people is a gift, which springs entirely from his own initiative; it is totally free. Yet this love is so passionate that God voluntarily binds himself in covenant to his chosen bride with a solemn oath of faithfulness.

This imagery also reveals sin as something inescapably personal. Breaking the covenant is not just an infraction of a "contract" made with God as supreme Legislator. It is *adultery*. "It is a blow which even pierces his heart as Father, as Spouse and as Lord."[4]

And in that day, says the LORD, you will call me, "My husband," and no longer will you call me, "My Baal." For I will remove the names of the Baals from her mouth, and they shall be mentioned by name no more. And I will make for you a covenant on that day.... And I will betroth you to me for ever; I will betroth you to me in righteousness and in

> justice, in steadfast love, and in mercy. I will betroth you to me in faithfulness; and you shall know the Lord.
>
> —HOSEA 2:16–20

God here likens Israel to a prostitute whose husband divorces her in anger, then restores her. The word "betroth" was used only for virgins. Hosea's choice of this word means that God does not just patch up the relationship but restores the freshness of the beginning. The bride is not destroyed but transformed! God's dealings with his bride are the ultimate in faithful love. The concluding phrase, "You shall *know* the Lord," alludes to intimate spousal union, as in Genesis: "Adam *knew* his wife Eve, and she conceived" (Genesis 4:1, emphasis added).

These passages deepen our understanding of God's love for his people, but at the same time they greatly elevate the significance of human marriage. Marriage is not just a social convention; it is a holy calling that is meant to bear witness to the character of God himself. This is why God "hates divorce" (see Malachi 2:14–16).

THE GREAT LOVE SONG

The pinnacle of spousal imagery in the Old Testament is the love song attributed to King Solomon, the Song of Songs. Ancient Jewish rabbis had great reverence for the mystical truths hidden in this book. As one said, "All the ages are not worth the day on which the Song of Songs was given to Israel; for all the writings are holy, but the Song of Songs is the Holy of Holies." He also held that "had not the Torah been given to Israel, the Song of Songs would have sufficed to guide the world."[5]

The Song is love poetry, a romantic ballad celebrating the love between a man and a woman. There is actually no mention of God in it. Because the language is "erotic," at various times Christians have even been forbidden to read it. Yet it is one of the most commented upon books in all Scripture. Throughout Christian tradition the Song has been a wellspring of mystical and spiritual theology.

Over the centuries there have been two main tendencies in interpreting the Song. The first approach, characteristic of the Fathers of the church, is allegorical: Every line applies in some way to Christ, the church or the individual soul. For example, the two breasts of the woman were sometimes seen as a figure of the two testaments of the Bible. The other approach, more typical of modern biblical scholars, is to take the Song in the purely literal sense as human love poetry that we should not attempt to allegorize.

John Paul II creatively unites these approaches, recognizing that the spiritual meaning does not deny or squash the literal meaning but rather gives it its full, rich value. The Song *is* celebrating the mutual attraction and one-flesh union of man and woman, which is a great and precious reality in its own right. But in God's plan this human reality also reveals to us something of God himself.

As the pope points out, the words of love in the Song focus on the human body. Indeed, the body is the source of the mutual fascination of the lover and his beloved. Yet the expressions of admiration do not stop there but involve the entire person. The lover calls his beloved "my sister, my bride," indicating that she is his equal and embracing her whole being with disinterested tenderness—the opposite of lust. He speaks of her as "a garden enclosed, a fountain sealed," recognizing her interior inviolability. As master of her own free choice she responds, "I am my beloved's and my beloved is mine," entrusting herself to him with complete freedom.

When this imagery is understood as a figure of the covenant between God and his people, the Song has much to teach us about the ardor of God's love and his profound respect for our freedom as persons.

THE CHURCH, THE BRIDE OF CHRIST

In the New Testament Saint Paul brings the spousal imagery to a new level, particularly in the passage from Ephesians on which John Paul II focuses: "Husbands, love your wives, as Christ loved the Church and gave himself up for her, that he might sanctify her" (Ephesians 5:25–26). Paul is referring to Jesus' death for us on the cross, the ultimate act of nuptial love. The cross is the consummation—the complete enactment in the flesh—of God's eternal covenant of love with his people. In pouring out his life for us, the Son of God espoused the church in an irrevocable bond. His gift is radical and total; it is all that God could give of himself to man.

This passage shows that the essence of the love of a husband is to lay down his life for his bride. What then is the essence of a wife's response? To *receive* that love with complete openness and *return* it with a reciprocal gift of self. Only when the gift is reciprocated is there a spousal union. Only when we recognize Jesus' act of love on the cross for what it is, and respond to it in gratitude and love, is our covenant bond with him made complete. The church "completes [the sacrament of Christ's redemption] just as the wife, in virtue of spousal love, completes her husband."[6]

The covenant between husband and wife is consummated and renewed in their physical union: The two become one flesh. Analogously, the Eucharist is the consummation and renewal of Christ's spousal gift of himself on the cross. It is his one-flesh union with his church. Each time we consume the Eucharist, we are invited to enter into personal "communion" with Christ, to receive his total gift of himself into the depths of our heart and respond by giving ourselves to him in love and gratitude.

The **spousal analogy** holds true not only for the church as a whole but for each of us as individuals, both men and women. John Paul II says:

> All human beings—both women and men—are called through the Church, to be the "Bride" of Christ.... The God who "first loved us" (1 John 4:19) and did not hesitate to deliver his Son out of love (see John 3:16) impels the Church to go "all the way" (see John 13:1) in love. And she is called to do so with the freshness of two spouses who love each other in the joy of giving themselves without reserve and in daily generosity.[7]

A spousal love for God does not preclude our having a human spouse. But it is a love that is total, that involves the surrender of our entire being.

The ultimate model of a bridal response to God is the Virgin Mary. When the angel Gabriel came to her at the Annunciation, she said: *Fiat*, "Let it be to me according to your word" (Luke 1:38). More than any other human being, Mary received the gift of God with complete openness, availability and gratitude. And her spousal communion with God was so total and so fruitful that she conceived and brought forth into the world the Son of God himself.

In an analogous way, we are all called to "conceive" God, to make room for him in our hearts. We are to say with Paul, "It is no longer I who live, but Christ who lives in me" (Galatians 2:20). In so doing we become like Mary a *theotokos*, a God-bearer.

To live this truth means to recognize that holiness is not something I *do* but something I *receive*. This truth is liberating! It takes the pressure off and frees us from the treadmill of religious self-effort. To deny this truth, on the other hand, leads to an overemphasis on programs and activities, which is a source of many of the problems in the church. We can organize all kinds of efforts "for Christ" without bothering to sit at his feet and receive what he actually wants to give. This severely limits our spiritual fruitfulness.

It should be noted that receptivity is not at all the same as passivity. Receptivity actually engages all our energy. It takes just as much skill for the running back to catch the football as for the quarterback to throw it. To listen well to a speaker involves just as much energy, attention and thought as does speaking. The more we, as members of the church, become receptive to the immensity of love God pours out on us, the more we become spiritually fruitful, and through us others are able to be born into and mature in God's family.

In this image of the wedding at Cana, the two spouses are not shown, whereas Jesus is in the foreground beside his mother, to show that Christ is the true Bridegroom and the church (personified by Mary) is his bride. The story of the wedding at Cana in John 2:1-11 symbolically points us to the Passion, in which Jesus consummates his marriage with the church by giving up his life for her on the cross.

STUDY TOOLS

Scriptures

Song of Songs

Isaiah 54:4–10

Ephesians 5:21–33

Church Teaching

> Christ is the Bridegroom because "he has given himself":
> his body has been "given," his blood has been "poured out"
> (cf. Lk 22:19-20). In this way "he loved them to the end"
> (Jn 13:1). The "sincere gift" contained in the sacrifice of
> the cross gives definitive prominence to the spousal mean-
> ing of God's love.... *The Eucharist* is... the *Sacrament of the
> Bridegroom and of the Bride.* The Eucharist makes present
> and realizes anew in a sacramental manner the redemptive
> act of Christ, who "creates" the Church, his body. Christ is
> united with this "body" as the bridegroom with the bride.
> (John Paul II, *On the Dignity and Vocation of Women,* 26)

General Audiences of John Paul II

July 28 to November 24, 1982.

Key Concepts

Sacrament: a visible sign of an invisible reality. In the more
specific sense, the seven sacraments are the signs instituted by
Christ and administered by the church, which signify and
confer divine grace.

Spousal analogy: the imagery in the Bible that presents God's
love for his people, and more specifically Christ's love for his
church, as that of a husband for his bride. This analogy
reveals the gratuitousness, ardor and faithfulness of God's
love. Human marriage not only reflects but participates in and

derives power from the mystery of God's spousal union with his people.

Questions for Reflection and Discussion

1. Choose one or two of the Old Testament spousal imagery passages quoted above to meditate on prayerfully. What does this tell you about what God is like and how he relates to you?

2. How do these same passages also elevate your understanding of the significance of human marriage?

3. Read 2 Corinthians 11:2, Ephesians 5:21–33 and Revelation 19:7–8; 21:1–4. In your experience, does the church recognize and live out her identity as a bride, or does she sometimes look more like a widow? How can the church more fully become what she is?

4. What does it mean that the church is called to be like Mary? Can you give some specific examples of how the church in twenty-first-century North America needs to imitate Mary?

5. Read the Song of Songs, the Book of Tobit and the pope's reflections on them (May 23 to June 27, 1984). How do these books celebrate the beauty of romantic love, while at the same time elevating it? How do they transform our understanding of sexuality?

Practical Application

Before going to Mass this week, prepare your heart by asking the Lord for an understanding of the spousal covenant he is renewing with his Bride in this celebration. During the Mass open your heart to receive Christ's personal and unconditional love.

Memory Verse

I will betroth you to me for ever; I will betroth you to me in righteousness and in justice, in steadfast love, and in mercy. I will betroth you to me in faithfulness; and you shall know the Lord.

—HOSEA 2:20

Chapter Seven

LIVING THE MYSTERY

As we saw in the last chapter, marriage was a sacrament "from the beginning"—a visible sign of the invisible mystery of God's nuptial love for his people. Like everything in human life, marriage was wounded by sin, but in Christ it has been healed and given a new significance. Marriage in Christ overcomes the disorder sin causes in us; but even more than that, it joins the *eros* of the natural attraction of the sexes to the *ethos* of the sacrificial love in which Christ gave himself for us. In Christ, marriage is transformed by grace and makes present in the world his own one-flesh union with his church.

The question to explore now is how, practically, spouses can live their marriage in a way that shares in and radiates that inexhaustible mystery of divine love.

A REFLECTION OF DIVINE LOVE

Let us look now at the whole passage on which this section of the pope's teachings is based.

> Be subject to one another out of reverence for Christ. Wives, be subject to your husbands, as to the Lord. For the husband is the head of the wife as Christ is the head of the church, his body, and is himself its Savior. As the church is subject to Christ, so let wives also be subject in everything to their

husbands. Husbands, love your wives, as Christ loved the church and gave himself up for her, that he might sanctify her, having cleansed her by the washing of water with the word, that he might present the church to himself in splendor, without spot or wrinkle or any such thing, that she might be holy and without blemish. Even so husbands should love their wives as their own bodies. He who loves his wife loves himself. For no man ever hates his own flesh, but nourishes and cherishes it, as Christ does the church, because we are members of his body. "For this reason a man shall leave his father and mother and be joined to his wife, and the two shall become one flesh." This [is a great mystery], and I am saying that it refers to Christ and the church; however, let each one of you love his wife as himself, and let the wife see that she respects her husband.[1]

—EPHESIANS 5:21–33

If there is any passage that makes people wince when they hear it in church, this is it! Women in particular may chafe at the injunction to "be subject to your husbands, as to the Lord."

The pope shows that the authentic interpretation of this profound text frees it from the distortions created by the history of disordered relations between the sexes, especially that of male oppression of women. In fact, when read correctly, this passage presents a vision of marital relations that completely overturns the model of domination and subservience caused by sin (see Genesis 3:16). And it offers a challenge that is just as daunting for men as for women—if not more so.

The **great mystery** refers to the union of Christ and the church, reflected and made present in the love of Christian husbands and wives. Paul uses the Greek word *agape* for this self-giving love. The reciprocal love of Christian spouses forms a life-giving communion of persons, which not only imitates but *participates in* the mystery of Christ's redemption.

"BE SUBJECT TO ONE ANOTHER"

As John Paul II points out, the key to properly interpreting Ephesians 5:21–33 is to read it in light of its introductory verse: "Be subject to one another out of reverence for Christ." The **mutual submission** of husband and wife is the foundation for their whole relationship. In love they defer to one another, and each puts the other's well-being ahead of his or her own. Paul describes it in another passage:

> [Be] of the same mind, having the same love, being in full accord and of one mind. Do nothing from selfish ambition or conceit, but in humility count others better than yourselves. Let each of you look not only to his own interests, but also to the interests of others.
>
> —PHILIPPIANS 2:2–4

The motivation for this mutual submission is "reverence for Christ"—that is, awe at the mystery of Christ's own love penetrating a person's heart.

So, in adding in the next verse, "Wives, be subject to your husbands, as to the Lord," Paul is in no way calling the wife to be a doormat. He is not instructing wives to relinquish their own desires or opinions merely to serve their husbands. On the contrary,

> Love excludes every kind of subjection whereby the wife might become a servant or a slave of the husband, an object of unilateral domination. Love makes the husband simultaneously subject to the wife, and thereby subject to the Lord himself, just as the wife to the husband.[2]

The corresponding instruction for men is "Husbands, love your wives, as Christ loved the church." How did Christ love the Church? Literally, "to the end" (John 13:1), by laying down his life for her on the cross. For a husband to love his wife in that way means his total affirmation of her as a person and his constant willingness to give every last drop of his life for her.

Paul could not have set a higher standard. How can any earthly husband manage to live up to it? Only by recognizing Christ's self-gift on the cross as not only a model for imitation but a reality from which he can draw life and empowerment.

In the exchange of love the husband and wife are equal, yet their roles are not identical. Paul speaks of the husband as "head of his wife, as Christ is the head of the church." In what does this headship consist? The pope describes it this way:

> [T]he husband is above all, *he who loves*, and the wife, on the other hand, is *she who is loved*.... [T]he wife's submission to her husband, understood in the context of the entire passage…, signifies above all the "experiencing of love."

In other words, the husband takes the initiative in self-emptying love. The wife receives and responds to his gift, so that the two are "mutually interpenetrated, spiritually belonging to one another."[3]

This does not mean that the differences between them are erased. They submit to one another *as* men and women— with all of their uniqueness as body persons.

INNOVATION IN CHRIST

The pope further develops this interpretation of Ephesians 5 in his apostolic letter *On the Dignity and Vocation of Women*.[4] He observes that although Paul's way of speaking is rooted in the customs of his time, the idea of "mutual submission" was revolutionary—and that even today its implications have yet to be realized in the relations between men and women.

> In relation to the "old" this is evidently something "new": it is an innovation of the Gospel.... The "innovation" of Christ is a fact: it constitutes the unambiguous content of the evangelical message and is the result of the redemption. However, the awareness that in marriage there is mutual "subjection of the spouses out of reverence for Christ," and not just that of the wife to the husband, must gradually establish itself in hearts, consciences, behavior and customs. This is a call which from that time onwards does not cease to challenge succeeding generations; it is a call which people have to accept ever anew. St. Paul not only wrote: "In Christ Jesus... there is no more man or woman," but also wrote: "There is no more slave or freeman." Yet how many generations were needed for such a principle to be realized in the history of humanity through the abolition of slavery! And what is one to say of the many forms of slavery to which individuals and peoples are subjected, which have not yet disappeared from history?
>
> But *the challenge presented by the "ethos"* of the redemption is clear and definitive. All the reasons in favor of the "subjection" of woman to man in marriage must be understood in the sense of a "mutual subjection" of both "out of reverence for Christ." The measure of true spousal love finds its deepest source in Christ, who is the Bridegroom of the Church, his Bride.[5]

While previous church teaching did not highlight this mutual authority of husband and wife, John Paul II sees it as a **development of doctrine**—that is, an aspect of revelation that is now being understood more fully than in previous times, through the grace of the Holy Spirit. Mutual submission does not contradict previous teaching, which affirmed that wives need to submit to their husbands; rather it deepens and elaborates it (in accord with Scripture) by adding that husbands also need to submit to their wives.

The ultimate basis for this teaching is an understanding of the human person that is grounded in the Holy Trinity. Just as among the divine Persons there is a single purpose of love that moves them, so married couples are called to grow in love, understanding and mutual deference such that they share a common will.

TRUTH IN THE LANGUAGE OF THE BODY

In the Western Christian understanding of marriage, the couple themselves are the ministers of the sacrament. Their words of consent—"I take you as my wife," "I take you as my husband"—create the marriage. The priest is merely a qualified witness.[6] The marriage becomes indissoluble when it is consummated in sexual union, in which the couple enact their total self-giving in the **language of the body** and become fully and truly one flesh (see Genesis 2:24; Ephesians 5:31).

The "language of the body" is the pope's term for the ability of the body to express self-giving love. He is not simply referring to "body language," by which someone's posture can communicate feelings like "I'm shy" or "I'm mad at you." He is pointing to the fact that the body is capable of expressing and enacting the deepest truths of the heart. The body is also capable of speaking falsely. Think, for instance, of the smile of an employee who is actually thinking about how to undermine a coworker's position.

Like the union between God and his people, the union of husband and wife is an objective fact expressed in the language of the body, which must then be lived out in all their daily interactions. When God made a covenant with the people of Israel, they swore fidelity to him on their very lives (see Exodus 24:7–8). In the same way, a man and woman who choose to marry bind themselves, both in their free consent and in their sexual union. They swear fidelity; they promise openness to children; they promise their whole selves. In so doing they create an unbreakable covenant bond. In their sexual union their bodies speak the truth of this covenant, echoing God's words of betrothal to Israel and Christ's words of love for his bride spoken from the cross.

Once the covenant is made, the couple continually are called to personalize it, to make it their own through a myriad of gestures of love that are unique to them as a couple.[7] If they consistently affirm the truth of their covenant through love and mutual submission expressed in the language of the body, then the covenant deepens and is strengthened. On the other hand, if they fail to speak truthfully in the language of the body, then concupiscence reigns, and they reduce one another to objects for self-gratification rather than persons worthy of love.

How Does This Apply to My Marriage?

As the pope knows, having personally counseled hundreds of engaged and married couples, there are as many ways of living out mutual submission as there are couples. All good marriages manifest some version of mutual submission. If the husband and wife communicate sincerely and really love one another, they will defer to one another.

Take the case of a couple running a household. To some degree they will have to delegate tasks to one another, based on temperament and mutual gifts. The way they divide tasks might differ from our typical assumptions based on family background and culture.

Other issues are too important to delegate—for example, raising children. On some issues the couple will disagree. In these cases they need to communicate, pray, listen (on both sides!) and come to a mutual decision. Sometimes this will require one spouse to yield to the other. But if the love is mutual, it will not always be the same person who gives way.

There is no doubt that the standard set by Ephesians 5 is a great challenge that confronts the deeply rooted selfish tendencies of our fallen nature. We all know marriages where "the two become one"—and then spend their time fighting over which one! In other marriages a long-term imbalance in "submission" on one side or the other can lead to simmering resentment beneath the surface. In still others the temptation is to withdraw emotionally and be resigned to polite coexistence in order to avoid painful confrontations.

These challenges are the very things that make marriage a powerful channel of grace for those who are open to it. Through conflicts and misunderstandings, the spouses can come to recognize their inability to love as God loves and their desperate need for Christ's redeeming grace. It is when their failures drive them to Christ in humble prayer that spouses can begin to experience his cross as a power at work in their lives. The Holy Spirit then gives them the grace to do what they cannot do on their own: to turn back to each other again and again, sincerely asking and granting forgiveness, thus gradually overcoming any hardness of heart toward one another. The cross of marriage is its glory!

But what of marriages where only one spouse seems to be interested in striving to live out God's original intention? In these cases, too, Christ's love and the powerful grace of the sacrament are available. If a wife, for example, perseveres in lovingly deferring to her husband, while upholding both her own and his dignity, she may discover her own need to be purified from habits of self-righteousness or judgment. And in time she may be surprised to find a softening in her husband as well.

Or if a husband begins to take leadership by serving, showing his reverence for his wife through daily gestures of tenderness and respect, he may be gradually freed from his own tendencies toward self-centeredness, and find his wife more open and receptive to his love. Even in the difficult circumstance where a marriage fails, those who turn to Christ will experience the healing of their wounds and the divine love that alone can satisfy the deepest needs of their heart.

God continually calls spouses, through the grace of the sacrament, to grow in love and fidelity. They need patience, since no marriage will be perfect this side of eternity. Even tiny steps on the part of one spouse are pleasing to God and will bear fruit in the long run. The language of the body matures over the course of a lifetime, through a couple's growing recognition of and reverence for the presence of God in each other (see 1 Thessalonians 4:3–7).

As the *Catechism* observes (#1613), the church has always seen great significance in Jesus' presence at the wedding at Cana, whereby he confirmed the goodness of marriage and proclaimed that from then on it would be a powerful sign of his presence. Some couples have quoted the words of the Gospel on their wedding program: "Jesus also was invited to the marriage" (John 2:2). Those who invite Jesus into their marriage, from their prenuptial preparations to their wedding day and throughout the years, will find the grace they need to mature and to experience the mystery of Christ's love revealed through their bodies.

Mutual submission is part of what is "new" about Christian marriage, but it is also very old. It is God's original plan for the way that men and women (and all humanity) are called to relate—without the antagonism created by domination and subservience. The restoration of this reality in Christian marriage is a sacramental sign of the new creation, a sign of hope for humanity as a whole.

The world needs to see that love is real and that the Triune God is its author. God calls all Christians—married, single and celibate—to live in and bear witness to that love.

The Holy Family exemplifies the loving communion and mutual submission to which all Christian spouses are called.

STUDY TOOLS

Scriptures
Genesis 2:21–25
The Book of Tobit
Ephesians 5:21–33

Church Teaching

> How can I ever express the happiness of a marriage joined by the Church, strengthened by an offering, sealed by a blessing, announced by angels, and ratified by the Father? …How wonderful the bond between two believers, now one in hope, one in desire, one in discipline, one in the same service! They are both children of one Father and servants of the same Master, undivided in spirit and flesh, truly two in one flesh. Where the flesh is one, one also is the spirit. (*CCC*, #1642, quoting Tertullian)

General Audiences of John Paul II

December 1, 1982, to July 4, 1984. You may also want to read the pope's apostolic letter *On The Dignity and Vocation of Women*, in *Theology of the Body,* pages 443–92.

Key Concepts

Development of doctrine: a progressively deeper understanding of the divine revelation that has been entrusted to the church in Scripture and Tradition.

Great mystery: the nuptial covenant between Christ and the church, reflected in the relationship of Christian spouses.

Language of the body: the way a person "speaks" through the gestures and actions of the body, which can communicate either truth or lies. This communication is deeper than "body language" in the psychological sense.

Mutual submission: the exercise of authority by husband and wife in marriage as mutual deference out of reverence for Christ.

Questions for Reflection and Discussion

1. Can you think of some examples of the ways in which a person expresses either truths or lies through the body?

2. As you prayerfully reflect on Ephesians 5:21–33, what insights does this passage give you about Christ's love for us?

3. If you are married, in what ways does this passage challenge you? Considering "mutual submission," what specific changes might the Lord be calling you to make in the way you relate to your spouse?

4. If you are single, what implications does the teaching on mutual submission have for your relationships in your family, at work and in other settings? In what specific ways are you called to reflect Christ's love to those around you?

5. Read the prayer of Tobias and Sarah (see Tobit 8:5–8). What does this passage say to you about the connection between God's love and human marriage?

6. Whether you are single or married, divorced or widowed, what steps can you take to open yourself more fully to Christ's love and allow him to fill your deepest needs?

Practical Application

If you are married, look for one specific way that you can let go of self and submit to your spouse in love each day—even if he or she does not submit to you. If you are single, look for one specific way you can yield to the wishes of another person in love each day—even if you don't feel like it.

Memory Verse

Be subject to one another out of reverence for Christ.

—EPHESIANS 5:21

Chapter Eight

LOVE IS FRUITFUL

If you have followed the theology of the body with enthusiasm so far, it may be at this point that you come to a stumbling block. It is well-known that only a small minority of Catholic couples accept and abide by the church's teaching on openness to life and the prohibition of contraception. Why, many people honestly wonder, does the church continue to insist on this outdated moral stricture in the face of such widespread noncompliance? Doesn't she risk digressing from the message of God's love and alienating the very people to whom she wants to appeal?

Yet for John Paul II, it is precisely at this point that the theology of the body comes to its culmination. Everything he has said so far points to the vital significance of the link between the union of spouses and the generation of new life. This **inseparable connection** is, literally, the crux of the theology of the body. It is where the horizontal (human spousal love) meets the vertical (God's creative power).

The theology of the body helps us to recognize that this connection is not accidental but is at the heart of God's great plan by which human beings image the Holy Trinity. The one-flesh union of husband and wife becomes "incarnate" in a child conceived and lovingly accepted, in a way that reflects the eternal procession of the Holy Spirit from the communion between the Father and the Son.[1]

In order to explore the pope's teaching on this topic with sincere and open minds, let us look briefly at the developments leading up to our current situation.

HUMANAE VITAE: RESPONSE TO A CRISIS

Until a few generations ago the unanimous teaching of all Christian churches—Catholic, Protestant and Orthodox—was that contraception was morally evil. Only in the twentieth century did this consensus begin to break down, due to factors such as the fear of overpopulation, the invention of more reliable methods of birth control and changes in the economic and social roles of women. Because of these developments and intense public advocacy (especially by Margaret Sanger, the founder of Planned Parenthood) in 1930 the Anglican Church became the first to reverse its position. Other mainline churches soon followed suit. The Catholic Church, in contrast, reaffirmed its traditional teaching in Pope Pius XI's 1930 encyclical *Casti connubii*.

A new crisis was triggered in the 1960s by the development of the birth control pill. Some Catholic doctors and theologians began to argue that the pill was "natural" and should be approved. Many advocated a revision of the church's doctrine. This pressure, coupled with the sexual revolution and the changes sweeping through the post-Vatican II church, created a climate of expectation that the teaching would be changed.

But in this, as in other matters, the successor of Peter remained a rock, just as Jesus called him to be (see Matthew 16:18). In 1968 Pope Paul VI stunned observers worldwide by issuing the encyclical *Humanae vitae* ("Of Human Life"), in which he reiterated the church's prohibition of all forms of contraception.[2] The encyclical sparked a firestorm of debate and open dissent. Many lay Catholics were dismayed by the controversy and tuned out. Many priests and catechists stopped preaching and teaching about sexual morality. Just as the sexual revolution exploded throughout the Western world, the church seemed to lose its voice on this subject. The result has been two generations of confusion about the church's teaching on sexual morality, especially among young people.

In the wider culture, as sex became unmoored from its intrinsic orientation to new life, it is no surprise that further disintegration ensued. The contraceptive mentality forged a direct path to the idea that sex is for pleasure and thence to the public acceptance of cohabitation, promiscuity, homosexuality, pornography and various perversions as normal expressions of human sexuality—developments that keen observers had foreseen years in advance. At the same time it paved the way for abortion, a further step in the drive to detach sex from its natural consequence.

The sexual revolution has left in its wake a fragmented society, characterized by deep disorientation about personal identity and the very meaning of life. Children born into this society, even those who are loved by their parents, cannot help but be affected by the cultural mentality that fertility is a disease rather than a gift and that children are a burden rather than a blessing.

A PROPHETIC RESPONSE

Even before he was a cardinal in Poland, Karol Wojtyla was at the forefront of the effort to provide a new and deeper foundation for the church's teaching on sexual morality. His book *Love and Responsibility*, written in 1960, approached the topic of sex and marriage from a fresh and unique angle. He was a member of the papal birth control commission established by Paul VI, though Communist authorities in Poland prevented his attending the group's final meetings.

When Wojtyla became pope he recognized with prophetic intuition that one of his highest priorities must be to deepen the biblical and philosophical underpinnings for the teaching in *Humanae vitae*. So he gave the church the theology of the body, which not only provides a new understanding of the person and the natural law but reveals the profoundly biblical roots of the church's sexual ethic. In his last series of talks on the theology of the body, the pope focuses on the heart of *Humanae vitae*'s teaching:

> [T]he Church... teaches that each and every marriage act...must remain open to the transmission of life.... That teaching, often set forth by the Magisterium, is founded upon the inseparable connection, willed by God and unable to be broken by man on his own initiative, between the two meanings of the conjugal act: the unitive meaning and the procreative meaning.[3]

Vatican II also taught the inseparable connection between these two meanings of the marital embrace—babies and bonding:

> The Church issues the reminder that a true contradiction cannot exist between the divine laws pertaining to the transmission of life and those pertaining to the fostering of authentic conjugal love.[4]

The inner logic of this "inseparable connection" begins to come clear when it is understood in light of the theology of the body. In their marital covenant, which is enacted in sexual union, a husband and wife give themselves in their totality as body persons. This gift includes their respective masculinity and femininity and the potential fatherhood and motherhood intrinsic to it. As the pope notes, "the human body speaks a language which it is not the author of."[5]

To join with another person in sexual union is to say in the language of the body, "I give myself to you totally." Any attempt to deliberately sterilize the sexual act, whether through contraception or sterilization or other means, falsifies the language of the body. It is to speak total self-giving, while actually *withholding* part of oneself—one's fertility—or refusing the fertility of the other. Therefore the gift of self is neither given nor received in its integrity, and the spouses —despite their best intentions—treat one another as objects rather than persons. The language of the body is not spoken in truth.

A NEW ACT OF CREATION

Scripture explicitly links the "knowledge" gained in spousal union with potential parenthood: "Adam knew his wife Eve, and she conceived and bore Cain, saying, 'I have gotten a man with the help of the Lord'" (Genesis 4:1). The Bible also alludes to the mysterious divine presence that occurs in every fertile act of sexual union: "Elkanah knew Hannah his wife, and *the LORD remembered her*; and in due time Hannah conceived and bore a son" (1 Samuel 1:19–20, emphasis added). In every conception of a human life, God performs a new act of creation: A new *person* comes into existence, a new face reflecting God's image in the world in a way it has never been reflected before.

To refuse this mysterious divine action is to shut the door in God's face and exclude him from the great mystery that is meant to image him to the world. Even more, because marriage is the primordial sacrament, the symbolic key in which God reveals his nuptial love for his people, to falsify the language of the body is to contradict the sacramental sign. It is to proclaim—even if unintentionally—that God's spousal love is *not* total and *not* life-giving.

As the pope observes, the "inseparable connection" between sex and procreation is not something peculiar to people of faith. It is part of the **natural law**, the capacity to discern good and evil, which God has written in every person's conscience. Human reason can discover the natural law, as long as reason is not clouded by the culture. And according to the natural law, as virtually every society until recent times has recognized, something is wrong when sex is deliberately severed from its life-giving potential. The Hindu leader Mahatma Gandhi, for instance, wrote:

> [Contraceptive methods are] like putting a premium on vice. They make men and women reckless.... As it is, man has sufficiently degraded woman for his lust, and [contraception], no matter how well meaning the advocates may be, will still further degrade her.[6]

A basic principle of the natural law is that if things are to prosper, they must be treated in accord with their nature. This holds true for a CD player, a rosebush, a racehorse—and for human sexuality. Everyone can recognize the truth of this principle. Faith is needed, however, to grasp fully the unfathomable goodness of the design for life-giving love with which God created us.

The more one comes to know God as a loving Father, whose heart overflows with love for us and whose plan is for our *flourishing*, the more one trusts that there is good reason even for those laws that don't immediately seem to make sense. This trust in our Creator must be at the foundation of every attempt to discern right and wrong, especially in those "hard teachings" of the church that cut so strongly against the grain of contemporary thinking.

NATURAL FAMILY PLANNING: WHAT'S THE DIFFERENCE?

For those sincerely striving to form their consciences according to the church's teaching, the question naturally arises: If contraception is morally illicit, why does the church allow the regulation of births through **natural family planning** (**NFP**)? Isn't this simply a different way of doing the same thing?

Like his predecessors, John Paul II emphasizes that there is a clear moral distinction between contraception and NFP. NFP accepts fertility as good and as integral to the person, rather than a disease to be suppressed. A couple who, for good reasons, abstain from intercourse during the wife's fertile periods do not falsify the language of the body by deliberately rejecting their potential fatherhood and motherhood. They either speak the language in truth through sexual union, or they find nonsexual means to express their mutual love. The language of the body is only spoken in truth.

On the other hand, a couple who use contraception violate the intrinsic connection between love and life that God has inscribed in their bodies. They thereby "act as 'arbiters' of the divine plan and they 'manipulate' and degrade human sexuality... by altering its value of 'total' self-giving."[7] In the language of the body, the difference between NFP and contraception is the difference between refraining from speech for a time and lying.

As philosopher Janet Smith has observed, some couples resist NFP because they realize that it would require a considerable change in their lifestyle. But the very fact that there is a major lifestyle difference is a clue that there is a significant moral difference, too.[8] The practice of periodic abstinence shapes the character of a couple, deepening their respect for one another as persons, strengthening their mutual love by fostering communication and nongenital forms of intimacy and thus helping them grow in chastity.

In other words, rightly understood and used, NFP is not just another method of "birth control." It is a practice that builds virtue and enables a deeper and more authentic love. By demanding self-mastery, it both challenges and strengthens a couple to rely on God's grace and thus live more fully "life in the Spirit."

Despite popular perceptions, the church's prohibition of contraception is not a demand that all Catholics raise enough kids to field a baseball team.[9] Echoing Vatican II, John Paul II encourages married couples to exercise "responsible parenthood" by thoughtfully discerning together the number and spacing of their children, taking into account "both their own welfare and that of their children, those already born and those which the future may bring" as well as "the material and spiritual conditions of the times."[10]

WHAT ABOUT REPRODUCTIVE TECHNOLOGIES?

The theology of the body also has implications for other aspects of marital chastity, which the pope later addresses in his encyclical *The Gospel of Life*. For example, many assisted reproductive therapies, such as artificial insemination or *in vitro* fertilization (and its newer variants), also tear apart the "inseparable connection" between the unitive and procreative meanings of marriage. Contraception aims at sex without babies; these **reproductive technologies** aim at producing babies without sex.

The bodily, reciprocal gift of self of husband and wife is the context willed by God for a couple to receive the gift of a child, and it is the only way of generating life that is in keeping with human dignity. To "produce" children through a laboratory procedure demeans the meaning and beauty of human sexuality and offends the dignity of children conceived in this manner. It contributes to a view of children as commodities to be acquired or discarded at will, rather than persons to be received as gifts. Even if the intentions of the couple are good, the use of reproductive technologies contributes to the utilitarian mentality that is at the heart of the culture of death.

The church does not oppose medical interventions that attempt to assist a normal sexual union in achieving fertilization such as certain drug therapies. Nor does it oppose medical procedures that aim to heal medical conditions that contribute to infertility, such as the NaPro Technology approach developed by the Pope Paul VI Institute for Human Reproduction.[11] In fact, the church highly commends these new developments, which are achieving increasing success. The church does oppose those methods that replace the marital embrace rather than helping it achieve its natural end.

Infertility can be a profound form of suffering for couples who experience it. It calls for compassion, understanding and support from other members of the body of Christ. Part of this support includes speaking the truth in love. Children are a gift from God, not a right to be sought by any means. Suffering borne in love can be a powerful instrument leading to fruitfulness in other ways: for example, in raising adopted children or in reaching out to others who are suffering.

The purpose of the church's teachings on sexual morality is not to burden couples with legal requirements but to set them free. Throughout his teaching Pope John Paul II insists that freedom comes through truth. It is only the full truth about the human person, about marriage, about love and about the gift of fertility that offers the happiness that comes through freedom.

The Father, Son and Holy Spirit created us to share in their life and love, to learn to make a sincere gift of ourselves in and through our relationships to others. Learning to do this is the work of a lifetime, and it is only possible through God's grace and mercy. Yielding to this work of God in us, in our marriages and in our families proclaims good news to the world and builds a culture of life.

"Whoever receives one such child in my name receives me; and whoever receives me, receives not me but him who sent me." — Mark 9:37

STUDY TOOLS
Scriptures
Genesis 1:26–28; 2:21–25; 4:1
Malachi 2:14–16

Church Teaching

> Children are the supreme gift of marriage and contribute greatly to the good of the parents themselves.... [W]ishing to associate them in a special way in his own creative work, God blessed man and woman with the words: "Be fruitful and multiply." Hence, true married love and the whole structure of family life which results from it, without diminishment of the other ends of marriage, are directed to disposing the spouses to cooperate valiantly with the love of the Creator and Savior, who through them will increase and enrich his family from day to day. (*CCC*, #1652, quoting *Gaudium et spes*, 50)

General Audiences of John Paul II

July 11 to November 28, 1984. You may also want to read Pope Paul VI's encyclical *Humanae vitae*, "Of Human Life," in *Theology of the Body*, 427–442.

Key Concepts

Inseparable connection: the unbreakable bond between the person-uniting and life-giving aspects of sexual union as intended by God.

Natural family planning (NFP): regulation of births through periodic abstinence from sexual union based upon the fertile signs of the woman. When rightly used, NFP can help the couple grow in chastity and mutual love.

Natural law: the understanding of good and evil based on human reason that is inscribed in every human person.

Reproductive technologies: medical interventions intended to achieve human procreation, many of which divorce the unitive and procreative meanings of human sexuality and demean the children conceived through them.

Questions for Reflection and Discussion

1. Read the words of Eve in Genesis 4:1. How do her words indicate that conceiving a child is a form of co-creation with God?

2. Look at the blessing of Rebekah in Genesis 24:60 and Psalm 127. Why do the Scriptures see children as a gift? What are some ways in which our own culture does not?

3. How is God's love for us always life-giving? Think of some examples from your own life where you have seen this.

4. What are concrete examples of ways in which married couples can help each other grow in holiness?

5. How is NFP intrinsically different from artificial contraception?

6. Read Romans 6:15–23. What is the difference between freedom based on the truth as the pope understands it and freedom as it is understood in the world around us?

Practical Application

Think of someone you know who is struggling to care for children in difficult circumstances. Thank the Lord for the gift that those children are to the world, and find a way to reach out to the parent in affirmation and practical support.

Memory Verse

> Lo, sons are a heritage from the LORD,
> the fruit of the womb a reward.
> Like arrows in the hand of a warrior
> are the sons of one's youth.
> Happy is the man who has his quiver full of them!
>
> —PSALM 127:3–5

Chapter Nine

BUILDING A CULTURE OF LIFE

Next to the Bible, one of the most popular books in history is J.R.R. Tolkien's trilogy *The Lord of the Rings*. Perhaps it is providential that Tolkien's novel, and the movies based on it, have gripped the imagination of two generations. In the genre of fantasy, the story unveils spiritual truths that are profoundly relevant to the world in which we find ourselves—and even to the theology of the body.

In *The Lord of the Rings* we see forces gathering for a battle of cosmic significance. Two cultures are pitted against each other. On one side is the Shire, a land steeped in the joys of home, kinship, friendship and ancestral ties—a world shaped by marriage and family. On the other side is Mordor, a land devoid of love, marriage, family and any personal commitments, a world whose goal is to demolish the Shire and everything it represents.

At the center of the war is a ring. This ring is not one that binds through covenant love but one that enslaves through lust, deceit and ambition. It is in fact the antithesis of a wedding ring. You could call it the "anti-marriage ring."

We, too, are in a world where forces are gathering for a great war—in our case, a culture war. We, too, are facing an "anti-marriage ring," in the form of an undermining of the marital bond and all that it safeguards: the family, the dignity of man and woman, the sanctity of human life. Our enemies in this battle are not human beings but "principalities,...powers,... the world rulers of this present darkness" (Ephesians 6:12), whose goal is nothing less than to destroy humanity.

The prophetic voice of Pope John Paul II has long recognized that the current threat to marriage and the family jeopardizes not only the life of individuals but civilization itself. As he puts it, "the future of humanity passes through the family."[1] The family is where a person learns what it means to be human. As goes the family, so goes humanity.

Divorce, contraception, abortion, cloning and same-sex marriage are all an attack on God's plan for life and love. And because marriage is the deepest symbolic revelation of God's relationship to us, these evils obscure the face of God. Thus we too are in the "Wars of the Ring." Like the characters in Tolkien's novel, each of us is called to play our part in bringing the *anti-marriage ring* to its ultimate destruction—in the fiery pit where it was forged—and to build instead a civilization founded on truth and love.

THE GOSPEL OF LIFE

In this perspective we can appreciate the intensity with which John Paul II has unceasingly spoken out in defense of human life and of the family. Ten years after completing his reflections on the theology of the body, John Paul II wrote his encyclical *The Gospel of Life*.[2] This letter is a prophetic call to all humanity, especially to Christians, to understand what a gift life is. It is a call to grasp the mystery that God not only created human life in his image but also suffered in order to re-create it. Entering into the pope's prophetic vision will both deepen our own conversion and help us to witness to the world, which is suffering so many woes as a result of sins against life.

The plea for human life does not come merely from the pope; it comes from God himself. In the ancient pagan world many cries and prayers were lifted up to the gods, appealing for the redress of human injustices. But in Israel there is something unique: It is *God himself* who pleads for justice and threatens to punish crimes against human rights. "Hear this, you who trample upon the needy, and bring the poor of the land to an end.... The LORD has sworn by the pride of Jacob: 'Surely I will never forget any of their deeds'" (Amos 8:4, 7). "Cease to do evil, learn to do good; seek justice, correct oppression; defend the fatherless, plead for the widow" (Isaiah 1:16–17).

The Gospel of Life is a prophetic document, because in it the pope speaks as an "ambassador for Christ"; God is "making his appeal through" him (see 2 Corinthians 5:20). Following the example of the prophets, the pope explicitly makes himself the voice of those who have no voice:

> We must also mention the mentality which tends to *equate personal dignity with the capacity for verbal and explicit*, or at least perceptible, *communication*. It is clear that on the basis of these presuppositions there is no place in the world for anyone who, like the unborn or the dying, is a weak element in the social structure, or for anyone who appears completely at the mercy of others and radically dependent on them....[3]

Concern for every individual, no matter how "useless" in the eyes of others, can only come from a transcendent vision of human life. As we have seen, the opening pages of Genesis unveil this transcendent vision: "The LORD God formed man of dust from the ground, and breathed into his nostrils the breath of life; and man became a living being" (Genesis 2:7). There is something Godlike about the man, who is animated by the very breath of his Creator and destined to share life with him forever. John Paul II says:

> Man is called to a fullness of life which far exceeds the dimensions of his earthly existence, because it consists in sharing the very life of God. The loftiness of this supernatural vocation reveals the *greatness and the inestimable value* of human life.... [D]espite its hardships, its hidden mysteries, its suffering and its inevitable frailty, this mortal life is a most beautiful thing, a marvel ever new and moving, an event worthy of being exalted in joy and glory.[4]

This testimony to the goodness of human life is the heart of *The Gospel of Life*. The encyclical gives particular attention to two opposite aspects of this truth: the heinousness of murder and the mystery of the life-giving death of Jesus.

"Cain, What Have You Done?"

The first chapter of *The Gospel of Life* is a meditation on Cain's murder of Abel, as told in Genesis 4:1–16. With this story the Book of Genesis begins to trace the long story of sin as it extends from Adam to Abraham and beyond. The most immediate consequence of the transgression of Adam and Eve is the sin "lying at the door" of Cain's heart, which ultimately gives birth to jealousy, conflict and fratricide.

The pope leads us to share in God's perspective on the horror of a human life unjustly taken:

> Like the first fratricide, every murder is a violation of the *"spiritual" kinship* uniting mankind in one great family, in which all share the same fundamental good: equal personal

dignity. Not infrequently the *kinship "of flesh and blood"* is also violated; for example when threats to life arise within the relationship between parents and children, such as happens in abortion or when, in the wider context of family or kinship, euthanasia is encouraged or practiced.[5]

Every human being is a *person*, created to reach fulfillment in a personal relationship to God, who cherishes this individual and has a plan for his or her full flowering in time and in eternity. No one but God can decide the moment of someone's death. When we step into that role, we replay the grasping for the knowledge of good and evil that brought death into the world in the first place. Just as God asked Adam, "Where are you?" (Genesis 3:9), he asked Cain, "Where is...your brother?" (Genesis 4:9). The pope observes:

> Cain does not wish to think about his brother and refuses to accept the responsibility which every person has toward others. We cannot but think of today's tendency for people to refuse to accept responsibility for their brothers and sisters. Symptoms of this trend include the lack of solidarity toward society's weakest members—such as the elderly, the infirm, immigrants, children—and the indifference frequently found in relations between the world's peoples even when basic values such as survival, freedom and peace are involved.[6]

The pope describes our contemporary society—pervaded as it is by these tendencies—as "the culture of death." The main feature of the culture of death is that it views death as a solution to problems: problems of population, of ethnic strife, of unwanted pregnancies, of physical suffering, even of anger among high school students. Cain, too, sees his brother's death as the only solution to his own feelings of jealousy and inadequacy—and then his own death as the solution to his guilt.

But God never sees death as a solution. He put a mark on Cain, "not to condemn him to the hatred of others, but to protect and defend him from those wishing to kill him, even out of a desire to avenge Abel's death."[7]

GOD SO LOVED THE WORLD

Human life is so precious that, through the death and resurrection of the Son of God, it became a gift of the Trinity by which humanity is reconciled and brought to share in divine life. In the mystery of the cross we see clearly the truth of the verses the pope quotes from the Book of Wisdom:

> God did not make death, and he does not delight in the death of the living. For he created all things that they might exist.... God created man for incorruption, and made him in the image of his own eternity, but through the devil's envy death entered the world, and those who belong to his party experience it.
>
> —WISDOM 1:13–14; 2:23–24

In Christ we see that the last word for human beings is not death but *life*. This is the heart of the new covenant between God and man, which Jesus enacted in his own body: "God so loved the world that he gave his only Son, that whoever believes in him should not perish but have eternal life" (John 3:16). Through his glorified and radiant body we have life anew. Death has been conquered, and human existence is transformed into a pledge of life with God forever.

The secret of this transformation is love. Jesus offered himself in such infinite love that he passed from time into the very heart of God himself—and brought us with him.

> Therefore, brethren, since we have confidence to enter the sanctuary by the blood of Jesus, by the new and living way which he opened for us through the curtain, that is, through his flesh, and since we have a great priest over the house of God, let us draw near with a true heart in full assurance of faith.
>
> —HEBREWS 10:19–22

As we begin to understand and lay hold of the immensity of God's gift of himself in Christ, we grow in appreciation of the undreamt-of dignity of human life. The pope, reflecting on the passion in the Gospel of John, writes:

> [T]here is yet another particular event which moves me deeply when I consider it. "When Jesus had received the vinegar, he said, 'It is finished'; and he bowed his head and gave up his spirit" (Jn 19:30). Afterwards the Roman soldier "pierced his side with a spear, and at once there came out blood and water" (Jn 19:34).
>
> Everything has now reached its complete fulfillment. The "giving up" of the spirit describes Jesus' death, a death like that of every other human being, but it also seems to allude to the "gift of the Spirit," by which Jesus ransoms us from death and opens before us a new life.
>
> It is the very life of God which is now shared with man.[8]

Jesus' victory over death reveals that there is no sin against life, no matter how great, that cannot be forgiven. There is no interior wound that cannot be healed, no broken self-image that cannot be restored, no habit of disorder in our thinking or relating that cannot be set right—all by the power of the infinite love pouring out from Jesus' pierced side. This is the message of hope that we are to bring to a world that has lost its bearings.

EVANGELIZING THE CULTURE

The power of the theology of the body is that it opens up for us God's vision, helping us to grasp what human life is all about. It is the sword of the Word of God "reforged": the truth about humanity revealed in Scripture from the beginning but now made accessible in a new way that is sharp, penetrating and powerful. Once we begin to understand the full implications of that vision, we awaken to the fact that we are called to bear witness to it by our lives.

As mentioned above, the battle for the future of humanity is not against human beings (that would be self-contradictory) but against the ancient serpent and his minions, the spiritual enemies who are behind every attempt to cheapen, degrade and destroy the dignity of the human person. Our primary weapons in this war are *truth* and *love*.

In our culture where so many people, including Christians, are unaware of the "great mystery" revealed in our bodies and the tremendous destruction that occurs when it is violated, we are called to be living icons of the truth that will set them free. If we are to bring the gospel of life to the heart of every man and woman, the first step is to allow our own selves to "be transformed by the renewal of our mind" (see Romans 12:2), by living it authentically. At the same time we must seek to make it penetrate every part of society—social, cultural, economic, political, educational—until every institution recognizes and upholds the immeasurable gift of human life.

John Paul II recognizes that we need courage for such witness.

> Faced with the countless grave threats to life present in
> the modern world, one could feel overwhelmed by sheer

powerlessness: good can never be powerful enough to triumph over evil!

At such times the People of God, and this includes every believer, is called to profess with humility and courage its faith in Jesus Christ, "the Word of life" (1 Jn 1:1).[9]

[This includes] the courage to *adopt a new lifestyle*, consisting in making practical choices—at the personal, family, social and international level—on the basis of a correct scale of values: *the primacy of being over having, of the person over things.*[10]

The family has a special role in this work. Quoting Paul VI, the pope emphasizes the irreplaceable witness of a family life that is suffused with the radiant joy and love of Christ:

The family, like the Church, ought to be a place where the Gospel is transmitted and from which the Gospel radiates. In a family which is conscious of this mission, all the members evangelize and are evangelized. The parents not only communicate the Gospel to their children, but from their children they can themselves receive the same Gospel as deeply lived by them. And such a family becomes the evangelizer of many other families and of the neighborhood of which it forms a part.[11]

It is natural to assume that the great forces of history, the movements that will shape the future of the world, are far beyond our influence. Not so! The seemingly small choices for good or evil made by seemingly insignificant people can have immense repercussions for the future. Every single person has a crucial and irreplaceable role, the importance of which will not be revealed until the drama is played out. God calls each of us to choose the good, even at risk to ourselves. He calls us to infuse every dimension of the cultural landscape with the good news of the gospel of life—tirelessly, perseveringly and with unshakable confidence in the ultimate triumph of the risen Lord.

STUDY TOOLS

Scriptures

Genesis 4:1–16
Psalm 139
1 John 1:1–4
Romans 8:28–29

Church Teaching

> *Why is life a good?* This question is found everywhere in the Bible, and from the very first pages it receives a powerful and amazing answer. The life which God gives man is quite different from the life of all other living creatures, inasmuch as man, although formed from the dust of the earth…*is a manifestation of God in the world, a sign of his presence, a trace of his glory* (cf. Gen 1:26–27; Ps 8:6). This is what Saint Irenaeus of Lyons wanted to emphasize in his celebrated definition: "Man, living man, is the glory of God." (John Paul II, *The Gospel of Life*, 34; emphasis in the original)

Writings of John Paul II

Read all or part of John Paul II's encyclical *The Gospel of Life*, in *Theology of the Body*, 493–582.

Questions for Reflection and Discussion

1. Prayerfully read Genesis 4:1–16. Why do human beings tend to see death as a solution to problems? What is God's response to this tendency?

2. Read and meditate on Psalm 139. How does this psalm show God's tenderness and intense personal interest in every human being?

3. Read the account of the crucifixion in John 19. What does it mean to say that Jesus conquered death?

4. Read Philippians 1:20 and Revelation 2:10. Why does bearing witness to the gospel of life require courage?

5. What new insights has the theology of the body given you about the dignity of human life?

6. What are some concrete ways in which God is calling *you* to build the culture of life?

Practical Application

Ask the Lord how you can share the good news of the theology of the body this week in a way that practically impacts the culture around you.

Memory Verses

> God did not make death,
> and he does not delight in the death of the living.
>
> —WISDOM 1:13

> God created man for incorruption,
> and made him in the image of his own eternity,
> but through the devil's envy death entered the world,
> and those who belong to his party experience it.
>
> —WISDOM 2:23–24

Notes

Introduction

1. This is the title of a recent book by marriage counselor John Gray: *Men Are from Mars, Women Are from Venus: A Practical Guide for Improving Communication and Getting What You Want in Your Relationships* (San Francisco: HarperCollins, 1992).

2. John Paul II, *The Redeemer of Man*, 25.

3. In the United States contact the John Paul II Institute for Studies on Marriage and Family, 415 Michigan Avenue, NE, Washington, DC 20017. Phone: 202-526-3799; Fax: 202-269-6090; Web site: www.johnpaulii.edu.

4. George Weigel, *Witness to Hope: The Biography of Pope John Paul II* (New York: HarperCollins, 1999), p. 343.

5. The text of the pope's addresses are also available in back issues of *L'Osservatore Romano*. When I quote from the pope's teaching, I include the date of the papal address in the corresponding endnote, so that readers can easily find it in either resource.

Chapter 1: Back to the Beginning

1. The Hebrew word *adam*, like *man* in English, can mean both "human being" and more specifically "male human being." One can infer the intended meaning from the context.

2. John Paul II, *The Theology of the Body: Human Love in the Divine Plan* (Boston: Pauline Books and Media, 1997), February 20, 1980, p. 76.

Chapter 2: Original Humanity

1. See the *Catechism of the Catholic Church*, #390.
2. Medical and psychological evidence confirms the fact that, although there may be genetic predisposing factors, homosexuality is not a genetically determined or unchangeable condition. See the statement by the Catholic Medical Association on "Homosexuality and Hope," available at www.cathmed.org.

Chapter 3: Fallen Humanity

1. See *Theology of the Body,* July 23, 1980, p. 126.
2. Author modified translation. *RSV* uses *thee.*
3. Translation modified. *RSV* uses *thou gavest.*
4. Pope John Paul II, *On the Dignity and Vocation of Women*, 10, in *Theology of the Body,* p. 456.
5. *Exsultet*, from the English translation of *The Roman Missal*, 2ⁿᵈ typical edition (New York: Catholic Book Publishing, 1985).
6. Translation modified. *RSV* uses *thy.*

Chapter 4: Redeemed Humanity

1. *Theology of the Body,* October 29, 1980, p. 167, emphasis added.
2. *Theology of the Body,* October 29, 1980, p. 167.
3. *Theology of the Body,* November 5, 1980, p. 171.
4. *Theology of the Body,* November 12, 1980, p. 171.
5. *Theology of the Body,* November 12, 1980, p. 172.
6. See *Theology of the Body,* April 1, 1981, p. 213.
7. *Theology of the Body,* December 3, 1980, p. 176.
8. *Theology of the Body,* March 18, 1981, p. 209.

Chapter 5: Glorified Humanity

1. *Theology of the Body,* December 9, 1981, p. 242.
2. *Theology of the Body,* December 9, 1981, p. 242.

Chapter 6: Marriage: The Primordial Sacrament

1. *Theology of the Body,* September 8, 1982, pp. 321–22.
2. *Theology of the Body,* October 20, 1982, p. 339.
3. *Theology of the Body,* September 22, 1982, pp. 327–328.
4. *Theology of the Body,* January 12, 1983, p. 358.
5. Rabbi Aqiba (c. A.D. 135), cited in Marvin H. Pope, *Song of Songs: A New Translation with Introduction and Commentary,* Anchor Bible (Garden City, NY: Doubleday, 1977), pp. 19, 92.
6. *Theology of the Body,* October 13, 1982, p. 338.
7. John Paul II, general audience of February 7, 2001.

Chapter 7: Living the Mystery

1. Translation slightly modified. *RSV* says, "This mystery is a profound one."
2. *Theology of the Body,* August 11, 1982, p. 310.
3. *Theology of the Body,* September 1, 1982, p. 320.
4. The full text of this encyclical is printed in *Theology of the Body,* pp. 443–492.
5. *On the Dignity and Vocation of Women,* 24, in *Theology of the Body,* pp. 478–479. All emphasis is in the original.
6. Eastern Catholics and the Orthodox have a slightly different view, in which the priest is the minister of the sacrament. The effect is the same, however.
7. See *Theology of the Body,* January 26, 1983, pp. 363–365.

Chapter 8: Love Is Fruitful

1. In every analogy relating to God, even those revealed in Scripture, we have to keep in mind the fact that God infinitely transcends human realities. God is not in man's image, but man in God's.
2. The full text of this encyclical is printed in *Theology of the Body,* pp. 427–442.
3. Paul VI, *Humanae vitae*, pp. 11–12.
4. Vatican II, *Gaudium et spes*, p. 51.
5. *Theology of the Body,* January 19, 1983, p. 361.
6. Quoted in Christopher Wolfe, ed., *Same-Sex Matters: The Challenge of Homosexuality* (Dallas: Spence, 2000), p. 30.
7. John Paul II, *On the Christian Family in the Modern World* (*Familiaris consortio*), p. 32.
8. Janet Smith, *Contraception: Why Not?* audiocassette, available free from One More Soul, 1-800-307-7685.
9. Studies have shown that NFP, used consistently, has a higher rate of success at preventing pregnancy than either condoms or the pill. See Robert A. Hatcher, *Contraceptive Technology*, 17th revised ed. (New York: Irvington Press, 1998).
10. *Theology of the Body,* August 1, 1984, p. 393, quoting Vatican II, *Gaudium et spes*, p. 50.
11. The Pope Paul VI Institute is located in Omaha, Nebraska. Phone 402-390-6600 or visit www.popepaulvi.com.

Chapter 9: Building a Culture of Life

1. *On the Christian Family in the Modern World*, p. 86.
2. The full text of this encyclical is printed in *Theology of the Body,* pp. 493–582.
3. *The Gospel of Life,* p. 19, in *Theology of the Body,* pp. 506–507.

4. *The Gospel of Life,* 2, 84, quoting Pope Paul VI, *Pensiero alla Morte* (Brescia, Italy: Istituto Paolo VI, 1988), p. 24, included in *Theology of the Body,* pp. 493, 559.
5. See *The Gospel of Life,* 8, in *Theology of the Body,* p. 499.
6. *The Gospel of Life,* 8, in *Theology of the Body,* p. 499.
7. *The Gospel of Life,* 9, in *Theology of the Body,* p. 500.
8. *The Gospel of Life,* 51, in *Theology of the Body,* p. 533.
9. *The Gospel of Life,* 29, in *Theology of the Body,* p. 515.
10. *The Gospel of Life,* 98, in *Theology of the Body,* p. 569.
11. *On the Christian Family in the Modern World*, p. 52.

RESOURCES FOR FURTHER STUDY

Related Works of Pope John Paul II

Evangelium Vitae (The Gospel of Life). Boston: Pauline, 1995.

Familiaris Consortio (The Role of the Christian Family in the Modern World). Boston: Pauline, 1981.

Letter to Families. Boston: Pauline, 1994.

Love and Responsibility, revised edition. H. T. Willets, trans. San Francisco: Ignatius, 1993.

Mulieris Dignitatem (On the Dignity and Vocation of Women). Boston: Pauline, 1988.

The Theology of the Body: Human Love in the Divine Plan. Boston: Pauline, 1997.

Introductions to the Theology of the Body

Hogan, Richard M. and John M. Levoir. *Covenant of Love: Pope John Paul II on Sexuality, Marriage, and Family in the Modern World*. San Francisco: Ignatius, 1992.

Shivanandan, Mary. *Crossing the Threshold of Love: A New Vision of Marriage*. Washington: Catholic University of America Press, 1999.

West, Christopher. *Theology of the Body Explained: A Commentary on John Paul II's "Gospel of the Body."* Boston: Pauline, 2003.

West, Christopher. *Theology of the Body for Beginners*. Wynnewood, Penn.: Ascension, 2004. This is the most readable popular introduction to the theology of the body.

Theology of the Body Applied to Moral Issues
Schu, Walter J. *The Splendor of Love*. Hartford, Conn.: New Hope, 2003.

West, Christopher. *Good News About Sex and Marriage: Answers to Your Honest Questions About Catholic Teaching*. Cincinnati: Servant Books, 2000. This book contains a helpful list of educational and referral resources on a variety of issues related to sex, marriage and family.

Marriage and Family
Burke, Cormac. *Covenanted Happiness: Love and Commitment in Marriage*. San Francisco: Ignatius, 1990.

Hahn, Kimberly. *Life-Giving Love: Embracing God's Beautiful Design for Marriage*. Cincinnati: Servant Books, 2001.

von Hildebrand, Alice. *By Love Refined: Letters to a Young Bride*. Manchester, N.H.: Sophia, 1998.

von Hildebrand, Dietrich. *Marriage: The Mystery of Faithful Love*. Manchester, N.H.: Sophia, 1997.

Sexual Morality

Grabowski, John. *Sex and Virtue: An Introduction to Sexual Ethics*. Washington: Catholic University of America, 2003.

Harvey, John F. *The Truth About Homosexuality: The Cry of the Faithful*. San Francisco: Ignatius, 1996.

Kippley, John F. *Sex and the Marriage Covenant: A Basis for Morality*. Cincinnati: Couple to Couple League International, 1991.

Lawler, Ronald et al. *Catholic Sexual Ethics: A Summary, Explanation, and Defense*, revised ed. Huntington, Ind.: Our Sunday Visitor, 1998.

Quay, Paul M. *The Christian Meaning of Human Sexuality*. San Francisco: Ignatius, 1988.

Smith, Janet. *Contraception: Why Not?* Audiocassette, available free from One More Soul, 1-800-307-7685.

Smith, Janet. *Why* Humanae Vitae *Was Right: A Reader*. San Francisco: Ignatius, 1993.

Chastity for Teens and Young Adults

Bonacci, Mary Beth. *Real Love: Answers to Your Questions on Dating, Marriage and the Real Meaning of Sex*. San Francisco: Ignatius, 1996.

Evert, Jason. *If You Really Loved Me: 100 Questions on Dating, Relationships and Sexual Purity*. Cincinnati: Servant Books, 2003.